Seed Saving

Master the Art of Seed Saving

(Grow the Perfect Vegetables Fruits Herbs and Flowers for Your Garden)

James Yeager

Published By **Jenna Olsen**

James Yeager

All Rights Reserved

Seed Saving: Master the Art of Seed Saving (Grow the Perfect Vegetables Fruits Herbs and Flowers for Your Garden)

ISBN 978-1-7781779-6-5

No part of this guidebook shall be reproduced in any form without permission in writing from the publisher except in the case of brief quotations embodied in critical articles or reviews.

Legal & Disclaimer

The information contained in this book is not designed to replace or take the place of any form of medicine or professional medical advice. The information in this book has been provided for educational & entertainment purposes only.

The information contained in this book has been compiled from sources deemed reliable, and it is accurate to the best of the Author's knowledge; however, the Author cannot guarantee its accuracy and validity and cannot be held liable for any errors or omissions. Changes are periodically made to this book. You must consult your doctor or get professional medical advice before using any of the suggested remedies, techniques, or information in this book.

Upon using the information contained in this book, you agree to hold harmless the Author from and against any damages, costs, and expenses, including any legal fees potentially resulting from the application of any of the information provided by this guide. This disclaimer applies to any damages or injury caused by the use and application, whether directly or indirectly, of any advice or information presented, whether for breach of contract, tort, negligence, personal injury, criminal intent, or under any other cause of action.

You agree to accept all risks of using the information presented inside this book. You need to consult a professional medical practitioner in order to ensure you are both able and healthy enough to participate in this program.

Table Of Contents

Chapter 1: Seed Saving 1

Chapter 2: Comprehensive Guide to Seed Saving 13

Chapter 3: Harvesting and Saving Seeds from 30 Herbs 44

Chapter 4: Techniques for Seed Saving and Unique Considerations 62

Chapter 5: Seed Saving Guide for Apple Varieties 68

Chapter 6: Seed Saving Guide for Stone Fruits 81

Chapter 7: Seed Saving Guide for Chestnuts 92

Chapter 8: Avocado Seeds 105

Chapter 9: Various Fruit, Tree, and Shrub Seeds 112

Chapter 10: A Comprehensive Guide for Home Gardeners 118

Chapter 11: Troubleshooting And Common Challenges 123

Chapter 12: Advanced Techniques Unveiled 129

Chapter 13: Fundamental Techniques for Retaining Seeds 137

Chapter 14: Plant Circle of Relatives Focus 147

Chapter 15: Troubleshooting and Common Mistakes 162

Chapter 16: Community and Global Impact 175

Chapter 1: Seed Saving

Embarking on the journey of seed saving is a profitable enterprise that connects you with the essence of gardening, permitting you to play a important position in keeping the legacy of plants. Whether you're a newbie gardener keen to discover the world of seeds or a seasoned horticulturist venturing into the art of seed saving, records the fundamentals and having the right tools and tool are vital for fulfillment.

In this entire manual, we are going to delve into the basics of getting commenced out with seed saving, imparting you with the know-how and resources to free up the functionality of your garden and add to the rich complex statistics of biodiversity.

Understanding the Basics of Seed Saving: A Primer for Beginners

1. Choose Open-Pollinated and Heirloom Varieties:

Before diving into seed saving, it is critical to pick plant life which is probably conducive to the approach. Open-pollinated and heirloom types are exquisite options due to the truth they breed real to type, which means that the seeds will produce plants with developments much like the decide plant. Hybrid types, but, won't showcase consistent inclinations in subsequent generations.

2. Isolate Crops to Prevent Cross-Pollination:

Many flowers are capable of bypass-pollination, where pollen from one plant fertilizes a few different. To hold the purity of seed types, it's far essential to isolate vegetation from capability flow-pollinators. This can comprise physical limitations, which incorporates netting or distance amongst flowers, relying on the precise dreams of the plant species.

3. Timing is Key:

Harvesting seeds on the right time is essential for a success seed saving. Give the seeds the opportunity to mature fully on the plant earlier than you harvest. Seeds are often equipped whilst the plant without a doubt begins to senesce or when the seed pods or fruit have dried and changed color. Timing varies among plant species, so it's miles important to investigate the unique necessities for each type you are saving.

4. Proper Seed Extraction:

After harvesting, extracting seeds efficaciously guarantees their viability. Techniques range depending at the plant. For a few, like tomatoes, clearly squeezing seeds out of the fruit can be sufficient. Others, at the side of beans or peas, require extracting seeds from pods. Thoroughly clean and dry the seeds before garage.

five. Drying and Curing Seeds:

Moisture is the enemy of stored seeds. To save you mould and keep seed viability, drying and curing are vital steps. Spread seeds in a single layer on a flat, breathable ground in a warmness, dry vicinity. Stir or turn the seeds often to make sure even drying. Once dry, keep seeds in hermetic packing containers in a groovy, darkish location.

6. Labeling and Record Keeping:

Accurate file-keeping is useful for seed savers. Label each batch of seeds with important statistics, along with the plant species, range, and the date of harvest. Additionally, maintaining a gardening mag can help music the achievement of specific types, imparting insights for future seed-saving endeavors.

7. Start Small and Gain Experience:

For beginners, starting small is beneficial. Experiment with a few smooth-to-hold seeds initially to assemble self warranty and advantage enjoy. As you grow to be more familiar with the approach, you could little by little expand your seed-saving endeavors to encompass a broader shape of plant kinds.

8. Community Involvement and Seed Exchanges:

Engaging with the nearby gardening network offers valuable insights and possibilities for seed change. Many groups host seed switch occasions where gardeners can percentage their saved seeds, increasing the variety in their gardens. Participating in the ones exchanges fosters a experience of community and connects you with professional seed savers.

Essential Tools and Equipment for Seed Saving: Building Your Arsenal

1. Garden Scissors or Pruners: Quality lawn scissors or pruners are vital for unique harvesting of seeds. Clean, sharp blades make sure a easy lessen, minimizing damage to the plant and the seeds.

2. Harvesting Bags or Envelopes: When amassing seeds, having dedicated bags or envelopes for each plant range permits save you bypass-infection. Label every bag with the relevant facts, alongside side the plant call and harvest date.

three. Drying Screens or Trays: Proper drying is a crucial step in seed saving. Drying video display units or trays permit air drift throughout the seeds, facilitating thorough drying and decreasing the threat of mildew.

four. Mesh Bags for Seed Heads: For plant life with small seeds or those who sincerely disperse, using mesh baggage to surround seed heads can capture seeds while allowing airflow. This prevents seeds from scattering in advance than you have got were given had been given a hazard to acquire them.

five. Seed Cleaning Screens: Seed cleansing presentations, available in various mesh sizes, assist separate seeds from chaff and debris. These video display units make the cleansing technique extra green and make sure that only possible seeds are saved.

6. Airtight Containers: Proper garage is crucial for keeping seed viability. Airtight bins, collectively with glass jars or plastic packing containers with tight-becoming lids, protect seeds from moisture and pests. Adding

desiccant packets allows control humidity within the bins.

7. Labels and Permanent Markers: Accurate labeling is paramount for prepared seed saving. Use climate-resistant labels and eternal markers to truely mark the plant species, variety, and harvest date on each discipline.

8. Gardening Journal or Notebook: Keeping a gardening journal presents a centralized location to document observations, strategies, and the achievement of different seed-saving experiments. This beneficial device aids in refining your seed-saving practices over the years.

9. Reference Materials and Guides: Invest in entire seed-saving publications and references to increase your knowledge. These property offer specific facts for wonderful plant kinds and provide troubleshooting suggestions for not unusual disturbing conditions encountered within the seed-saving manner.

10. Community Involvement: Connect with local gardening businesses, online forums, or seed-saving organizations. Networking with professional seed savers can offer guidance, tips, or maybe opportunities for seed exchanges. Learning from the collective reputation of a network complements your seed-saving adventure.

As you embark on the enriching adventure of seed saving, expertise the fundamentals and having the proper equipment and gadget are key to fulfillment. By incorporating the ones essential ideas and acquiring the crucial equipment, you not tremendous maintain the genetic form of vegetation but moreover actively make a contribution to the sustainability and resilience of your lawn and the wider environment.

The artwork of seed saving is a undying practice that empowers you to grow to be a steward of biodiversity, fostering a deeper reference to the cycles of nature and the flourishing life within your garden.

Comprehensive Guide to Vegetable Seed Saving:

Starting the adventure of vegetable seed saving is a profitable organization that not most effective empowers you as a gardener but moreover contributes to the sustainability and biodiversity of your garden. Here's an in depth manual on seed saving for severa vegetable organizations, which incorporates Solanaceae (Tomatoes, Peppers, and others), Leafy Greens (Lettuce, Spinach, Kale, and so on.), Root Vegetables (Carrots, Beets, Radishes, and so on.), and Crucifers (Broccoli, Cauliflower, Cabbage, and plenty of others.).

Tomato:

1. Variety Selection:

Choose open-pollinated or heirloom tomato kinds for seed saving.

Avoid hybrid types, as they will not produce authentic-to-type seeds.

2. Seed Extraction:

Scoop seeds from ripe tomatoes at the component of the gel.

Place the seeds and gel in a jar and permit fermentation for two-four days. This system removes the gel coating.

three. Cleaning and Drying:

Rinse the seeds thoroughly to get rid of ultimate gel.

Spread seeds on a show or paper towel to dry genuinely.

Store dry seeds in labeled envelopes or packing containers in a fab, dark region.

Potato:

1. Propagation:

Potatoes are typically grown from tubers, however if you need to increase from seed, gather seeds from the small surrender stop end result that form after flowering.

2. Harvesting Seeds:

Allow the potato plant to flower and produce small fruits.

Harvest the stop end result and extract the seeds.

three. Drying and Storage:

Air-dry the seeds thoroughly earlier than storing them in a cool, darkish region.

Note that potatoes are regularly propagated thru tubers in place of seeds.

Bell Pepper:

1. Harvesting Seeds:

Let bell peppers benefit their most ripeness on the plant.

Cut open the peppers and extract the seeds.

2. Cleaning Process:

Take out any dirt or chaff from the seeds.

three. Drying and Storage:

Dry the seeds on a plate or screen.

Store the cleaned seeds in hermetic containers in a groovy, darkish region.

Eggplant:

1. Variety Choice:

Go for open-pollinated eggplant kinds.

Seed from Hybrid types might not be right to the determine plant.

2. Harvesting Seeds:

Allow eggplants to really ripen at the plant.

Extract seeds from ripe eggplants.

Chapter 2: Comprehensive Guide to Seed Saving

Preserving the seeds of root greens is a satisfying and sustainable exercising that lets in you to preserve the proper tendencies of your preferred kinds. This whole guide will lead you through the precise way of saving seeds for various root vegetables, ensuring fulfillment and continuity to your garden.

Common Principles for Root Vegetables:

Biennial Growth: Many root greens are biennials, which mean they produce seeds in their 2d 12 months. Allow some flowers to overwinter for seed manufacturing.

Bolting and Flowering: Bolting is the herbal process in which the plant produces a flowering stalk. Allow a few vegetation to bolt and produce plants for seed improvement.

Harvesting Seeds Seeds are organized for harvest whilst the seed heads or pods flip brown and dry at the plant Collect seeds via lightly rubbing the seed heads or pods to release the seeds.

Cleaning Process: Take out any dust or chaff from the seeds.

Drying and Storage: Dry seeds very well on a display or paper towel Store smooth, dry seeds in classified envelopes or hermetic boxes in a groovy, darkish vicinity.

Specific Guidelines for Root Vegetables:

1. Carrot:

Biennial Nature: Carrots are biennials, producing seeds in their 2d year.

Leave some in the Ground: Allow a few carrots to overwinter for seed production.

Harvesting and Storage: Harvest brown, dry seeds. Clean and keep in categorized envelopes or hermetic packing containers.

2. Onion, Garlic, Leek:

Bulb Division: These are typically propagated through bulbs, however if grown from seed, harvest seeds from mature flower heads.

Drying and Storage: Air-dry seeds very well earlier than storing in a groovy, darkish location.

three. Radish, Beets, Fennel, Turnip, Rutabaga, Jicama, Daikon Radish:

Bolting Stage: Allow a few to accumulate the bolting level for seed saving.

Harvest and Storage: Harvest seed pods whilst dry. Clean seeds and keep in envelopes or containers.

4. Celeriac (Celery Root), Kohlrabi:

Biennial Growth: Similar to carrots, celeriac, and kohlrabi are biennials. Allow them to overwinter for seed manufacturing.

Harvesting Seeds: Harvest brown, dry seeds. Clean and shop in labeled envelopes or airtight boxes.

General Tips for Root Vegetable Seed Saving:

Variety Selection: Choose open-pollinated or heirloom sorts to maintain seed consistency.

Isolation Techniques: To save you move-pollination, separate precise sorts of the identical species.

Record Keeping: Keep positive records, noting planting dates, flowering durations, and any located traits.

Periodic Viability Testing: Test seed viability periodically with the beneficial aid of germinating a small sample to make certain they live feasible for planting.

By following the ones first-rate hints tailor-made to each root vegetable, you may now not simplest ensure a bountiful harvest however moreover make contributions to the resilience and kind of your lawn.

Comprehensive Guide to Seed Saving: Cruciferous Vegetables

Saving seeds from cruciferous greens is a satisfying and sustainable exercise that ensures the continuation of your selected kinds. This certain guide will take you thru the intricacies of saving seeds for various cruciferous vegetables, fostering fulfillment and variety for your lawn.

Common Principles for Cruciferous Vegetables:

Biennial Growth: Many cruciferous greens are biennials, producing seeds in their 2nd 12 months. Allow a few flowers to overwinter for seed manufacturing.

Bolting and Flowering: Bolting is a natural technique in which the plant produces a flowering stalk. Allow some flora to bolt and produce plants for seed improvement.

Harvesting Seeds Seeds are ready for harvest whilst the seed pods flip brown and dry at the plant. Collect seeds with the useful resource of lightly rubbing the seed pods to launch the seeds.

Cleaning Process: Remove any particles or chaff from the seeds.

Drying and Storage: Dry seeds very well on a screen or paper towel Store easy, dry seeds in categorized envelopes or airtight packing containers in a cool, darkish location.

Specific Guidelines for Cruciferous Vegetables:

1. Broccoli, Cauliflower, Cabbage, Brussels Sprouts:

Biennial Characteristics: Often biennial, flowering and producing seeds in the second 12 months.

Overwintering Plants: Leave a few plant life inside the ground through wintry weather for flowering and seed manufacturing.

Harvesting Seeds: Harvest mature seed pods while dry at the plant.

Drying and Cleaning: Allow seeds to dry similarly after harvesting. Clean seeds with the useful resource of winnowing or using video display units.

Storage: Store clean seeds in labeled envelopes or airtight containers in a groovy, dark vicinity.

2. Arugula, Bok Choy, Napa Cabbage, Turnip, Rutabaga, Collard Greens, Mustard Greens, Kale, Kohlrabi, Watercress:

Bolting and Flowering: Allow some plant life to bolt and convey plant life.

Harvesting Seeds: Collect dry seeds after flowering.

Cleaning and Storage: Remove particles and preserve smooth seeds in categorized envelopes or containers.

General Tips for Cruciferous Vegetable Seed Saving:

Variety Selection: Choose open-pollinated or heirloom kinds to hold seed consistency.

Isolation Techniques: To save you cross-pollination, separate one-of-a-type styles of the equal species.

Record Keeping: Keep particular records, noting planting dates, flowering periods, and any determined tendencies.

Periodic Viability Testing: Test seed viability periodically with the useful resource of germinating a small pattern to ensure they remain viable for planting.

By following those precise tips tailored to each cruciferous vegetable, you'll ensure the resilience and kind of your garden.

Here are a few preferred techniques for seed saving for not unusual veggies:

Choose Open-Pollinated Varieties: Open-pollinated sorts produce seeds which might be more likely to come returned decrease back actual to the determine plant. Avoid hybrid types for seed saving.

Isolate Different Varieties: Prevent pass-pollination by using manner of way of keeping apart extraordinary forms of the equal species. This can be achieved with the aid of using the use of spacing plants very well or the use of bodily obstacles like row covers.

Harvest at the Right Time: Allow quit result or veggies to truly ripen earlier than harvesting seeds. The seeds indoors want to be mature for a hit germination.

Bolting and Flowering: Understand the natural existence cycle of the plant. Many vegetation, particularly biennials, will bolt and bring flowers in advance than placing seeds. Allow some plants to undergo this method for seed development.

Seed Extraction: Properly extract seeds from the culmination or veggies. This can also contain fermentation, drying, or different precise strategies depending at the plant.

Fermentation (for a few end quit result like tomatoes): Fermentation allows to break down the gel spherical tomato seeds. Scoop seeds together with the gel into a box, permit it to ferment for some days, after which easy and dry the seeds.

Drying Seeds: Ensure seeds are thoroughly dry in advance than storing to save you mold. Use shows, paper towels, or different materials to facilitate drying.

Cleaning Seeds: Remove debris or chaff from the seeds. This may be completed through winnowing, sieving, or hand-cleansing.

Labeling: Clearly label your seeds with the plant call and the date of harvest. Good record-preserving is essential for a hit seed saving.

Storage: Store seeds someplace cool, dry, and darkish. Use airtight packing containers or labeled envelopes to preserve seeds prepared.

Viability Testing: Periodically check the viability of stored seeds thru germinating a small pattern. This ensures that the seeds are despite the fact that feasible for planting.

Understand Plant Families: Different plant life have wonderful seed-saving requirements. Understanding the households they belong to can offer insights into their specific goals.

Patience: Seed saving requires staying energy. It frequently includes watching for flora to go through their natural existence cycle to provide feasible seeds.

Remember, at the equal time as those strategies are fashionable, each plant may additionally moreover furthermore have precise requirements. It's important to investigate the precise needs of the veggies you're saving seeds from to make sure fulfillment

Tips, and Preservation Techniques For Successful Seed Saving For Various Common Vegetables:

Here are particular troubles, harvesting, processing, and garage suggestions, similarly to keeping tendencies for numerous common veggies:

Tomatoes:

Unique Considerations:

Tomatoes are frequently self-pollinating, but isolation can assist maintain purity.

Different kinds may additionally have particular traits like period, form, and taste.

Harvesting and Processing:

Harvest absolutely ripe tomatoes for seed extraction.

Ferment seeds for a few days to eliminate gel coating.

Dry very well earlier than storage.

Preserving Characteristics:

Save seeds from the nice-tasting and maximum sickness-resistant tomatoes to maintain favorable inclinations.

Lettuce:

Unique Considerations:

Lettuce has an inclination to bolt in warmth weather, primary to seed production.

Different kinds show off diverse leaf shapes, colorings, and textures.

Harvesting and Processing:

Allow positive flowers to bolt and bring seeds.

Harvest seeds on the identical time as fluffy and dry.

Winnow or sift seeds to put off debris.

Preserving Characteristics:

Save seeds from plant life with the popular taste, texture, and resistance to bolting.

Carrots:

Unique Considerations:

Carrots are biennials, requiring overwintering for seed production.

Different kinds offer various colors and flavors.

Harvesting and Processing:

Leave a few carrots inside the floor for overwintering.

Harvest seeds at the same time as brown and dry.

Clean and save in categorised envelopes.

Preserving Characteristics:

Save seeds from carrots with the favored colour, length, and beauty.

Broccoli:

Unique Considerations:

Broccoli is a biennial, requiring overwintering for seed production.

Different kinds can also have numerous head styles and sizes.

Harvesting and Processing:

Leave some plants inside the floor through winter.

Harvest mature seed pods even as dry.

Clean seeds and save in labeled envelopes.

Preserving Characteristics:

Save seeds from plant life with the preferred head trends and illness resistance.

Peppers:

Unique Considerations:

Pepper plants can bypass-pollinate, so isolation is essential.

Varieties variety in warm temperature levels, colorations, and shapes.

Harvesting and Processing:

Allow peppers to clearly ripen at the plant.

Extract seeds from ripe peppers.

Clean and dry seeds earlier than garage.

Preserving Characteristics:

Save seeds from the pepper flora with the preferred heat degree, shade, and taste.

Cucumbers:

Unique Considerations:

Cucumbers may additionally bypass-pollinate, so isolation is critical.

Varieties range period-sensible, shape, and flavor.

Harvesting and Processing:

Harvest mature cucumbers for seed extraction.

Scoop out seeds and ferment for some days.

Clean and dry seeds earlier than garage.

Preserving Characteristics:

Save seeds from cucumbers with the favored length, form, and taste.

Beans:

Unique Considerations:

Beans are frequently self-pollinating, but a few skip-pollination may additionally additionally moreover stand up.

Different kinds include bush and pole beans with numerous pod sizes and sunglasses.

Harvesting and Processing:

Allow beans to definitely mature on the plant.

Harvest dry pods for seed extraction.

Thoroughly dry seeds in advance than garage.

Preserving Characteristics:

Save seeds from plants with the desired pod period, color, and ailment resistance.

Zucchini:

Unique Considerations:

Zucchinis can also skip-pollinate, however isolation can prevent it.

Varieties fluctuate period-clever, color, and form.

Harvesting and Processing:

Harvest mature zucchinis for seed extraction.

Scoop out seeds and clean.

Dry seeds thoroughly earlier than storage.

Preserving Characteristics:

Save seeds from zucchinis with the favored length, color, and taste.

Onions:

Unique Considerations:

Onions are generally propagated via bulbs however can be grown from seeds.

Different types provide awesome bulb shades, sizes, and flavors.

Harvesting and Processing:

Allow a few onions to flower and bring seeds.

Harvest seed heads whilst dry.

Air-dry seeds in advance than storage.

Preserving Characteristics:

Save seeds from onions with the popular color, length, and taste.

Spinach:

Unique Considerations:

Spinach is a cool-season crop which could bolt in warmer weather.

Varieties can also range in leaf form, shade, and flavor.

Harvesting and Processing:

Allow a few spinach plant life to bolt and bring seeds.

Harvest dry, brown seeds via the usage of rubbing the seed heads.

Winnow or sieve to eliminate debris.

Preserving Characteristics:

Save seeds from spinach with the favored leaf developments and resistance to bolting.

Corn:

Unique Considerations:

Corn is wind-pollinated, and isolation is vital to preserve purity.

Different types offer severa kernel colorings, sizes, and flavors.

Harvesting and Processing:

Harvest mature ears for seed extraction.

Remove kernels and air-dry thoroughly.

Store dry seeds in labeled bins.

Preserving Characteristics:

Save seeds from corn with the favored kernel traits.

These problems, suggestions, and upkeep strategies are essential for a success seed saving, supporting you preserve the specific dispositions of your chosen veggies to your lawn. Adjustments may be wanted based to your precise developing situations and options. Happy gardening and seed saving!

Seed Saving Guide for 40 Beautiful Flowers

Flowers no longer simplest grace our gardens with beauty however additionally offer the opportunity to store and propagate their seeds, ensuring a non-stop cycle of blooms. Here's an extensive manual on seed saving for forty fascinating flowers, each with its unique characteristics.

1. Sunflower (Helianthus annuus):

Seed Saving:

Harvest seeds whilst the flower head droops and the back turns yellow.

Allow seeds to certainly dry on the top.

Rub seeds from the pinnacle and save in a groovy, dry area.

2. Rose (Rosa):

Seed Saving:

Collect rose hips in overdue fall once they flip vibrant crimson or orange.

Extract seeds from the hips, smooth, and air-dry.

Store seeds in a categorised, hermetic subject within the fridge.

three. Marigold (Tagetes):

Seed Saving:

Allow vegetation to vanish and form seed heads.

Harvest dried seed heads, damage them open, and gather seeds.

Store in a cool, dark area.

four. Tulip (Tulipa):

Seed Saving:

Allow tulip seed pods to mature after the petals fall.

Collect seeds from the pods, dry them thoroughly.

Store in a cool, dry vicinity.

5. Daisy (Bellis perennis):

Seed Saving:

Let the daisy plants dry at the plant.

Collect seed heads, dispose of seeds, and air-dry.

Store in a categorised envelope.

6. Lily (Lilium):

Seed Saving:

Allow lily seed pods to mature after flowering.

Collect seeds from the pods, air-dry, and hold in a fab vicinity.

Germination might also moreover take time; be affected individual.

7. Pansy (Viola tricolor):

Seed Saving:

Leave a few pansies uncut to supply seeds.

Harvest mature seed pods, extract seeds, and air-dry.

Store in a fab, dark area.

eight. Petunia (Petunia):

Seed Saving:

Allow spent plant life to shape seed pods.

Collect pods, extract tiny seeds, and air-dry.

Store seeds in a labeled envelope.

nine. Zinnia (Zinnia elegans):

Seed Saving:

Allow some zinnias to live at the plant till seeds form.

Harvest dried flower heads, collect seeds, and air-dry.

Store in a cool, dry location.

10. Poppy (Papaver):

Seed Saving:

Let poppy pods dry on the plant after flowering.

Harvest mature pods, extract seeds, and air-dry.

Store seeds in a labeled field.

eleven. Daffodil (Narcissus):

Seed Saving:

Daffodils commonly do not produce actual seeds; propagate through bulbs.

Allow leaves to wither glaringly, then enhance and divide bulbs.

12. Orchid (Orchidaceae):

Seed Saving:

Orchids often require specialized techniques for seed propagation.

Consult unique orchid species suggestions or are looking for expert recommendation.

13. Carnation (Dianthus):

Seed Saving:

Allow carnation plants to disappear and shape seed heads.

Harvest dried seed heads, extract seeds, and air-dry.

Store in a groovy, darkish location.

14. Gerbera Daisy (Gerbera jamesonii):

Seed Saving:

Allow spent vegetation to shape seed heads.

Harvest mature seed heads, extract seeds, and air-dry.

Store seeds in a labeled envelope.

15. Lavender (Lavandula):

Seed Saving:

Allow lavender flowers to dry at the plant.

Harvest dried flower spikes, take away seeds, and air-dry.

Store in a groovy, dark place.

16. Chrysanthemum (Chrysanthemum):

Seed Saving:

Allow chrysanthemum plant life to mature and shape seed heads.

Harvest dried seed heads, acquire seeds, and air-dry.

Store in a groovy, dark area.

17. Hydrangea (Hydrangea):

Seed Saving:

Hydrangeas frequently propagate via cuttings or layering.

Allow some vegetation to mature for capability seed formation.

Consult unique species hints for seed saving.

18. Peony (Paeonia):

Seed Saving:

Peonies often do no longer produce real seeds; propagation is generally through branch.

Divide peony clumps inside the fall.

19. Snapdragon (Antirrhinum):

Seed Saving:

Allow snapdragon flora to mature on the plant.

Harvest dried seed pods, gather seeds, and air-dry.

Store in a fab, darkish vicinity.

20. Cosmos (Cosmos bipinnatus):

Seed Saving:

Leave some cosmos flora on the plant till seeds shape.

Harvest dried flower heads, acquire seeds, and air-dry.

Store in a groovy, dry location.

21. Bleeding Heart (Dicentra spectabilis):

Seed Saving:

Bleeding hearts might also produce seeds after flowering.

Allow seed pods to mature, accumulate seeds, and air-dry.

Store in a groovy, dark vicinity.

22. Hollyhock (Alcea rosea):

Seed Saving:

Allow hollyhock plant life to disappear and form seed heads.

Harvest dried seed heads, extract seeds, and air-dry.

Store seeds in a classified envelope.

23. Black-Eyed Susan (Rudbeckia hirta):

Seed Saving:

Leave some black-eyed susans uncut for seed production.

Harvest mature seed heads, extract seeds, and air-dry.

Store in a cool, darkish location.

24. Dianthus (Dianthus caryophyllus):

Seed Saving:

Allow dianthus vegetation to vanish and form seed heads.

Harvest dried seed heads, extract seeds, and air-dry.

Store in a fab, darkish location.

25. Morning Glory (Ipomoea):

Seed Saving:

Allow morning glory plants to mature on the plant.

Harvest dried seed pods, accumulate seeds, and air-dry.

Store in a categorized location.

26. Foxglove (Digitalis purpurea):

Seed Saving:

Allow foxglove flora to shape seed pods after blooming.

Harvest dried pods, acquire seeds, and air-dry.

Store seeds in a fab, dark location.

27. Sweet Alyssum (Lobularia maritima):

Seed Saving:

Allow candy alyssum vegetation to disappear and form seed heads.

Harvest dried seed heads, extract seeds, and air-dry.

Chapter 3: Harvesting and Saving Seeds from 30 Herbs

Herbs now not handiest beautify the flavors of our dishes however furthermore make contributions to medicinal and fragrant abilities. To domesticate a sustainable herb lawn, knowledge the art work of seed saving is crucial. Here's a entire guide on how to harvest and store seeds from 30 numerous herbs:

1. Basil (Ocimum basilicum):

Seed Saving:

Allow basil plant life to bloom and visit seed.

Harvest dried seed heads, thresh to dispose of seeds, and air-dry.

Store seeds in a groovy, dry vicinity.

2. Mint (Mentha):

Seed Saving:

Mint has a bent to spread via rhizomes; seed saving is non-obligatory.

Allow some flowers to flower and shape seeds.

Harvest dried seed heads, collect seeds, and air-dry.

3. Rosemary (Rosmarinus officinalis):

Seed Saving:

Rosemary is frequently propagated through cuttings.

Allow a few plant life to flower and shape seeds.

Harvest dried seed heads, acquire seeds, and air-dry.

four. Thyme (Thymus):

Seed Saving:

Thyme won't produce adequate seeds; recall department.

Allow a few plant life to flower and form seeds.

Harvest dried seed heads, collect seeds, and air-dry.

5. Parsley (Petroselinum crispum):

Seed Saving:

Parsley is a biennial; it produces seeds within the second year.

Allow some plant life to flower and form seeds.

Harvest dried seed heads, acquire seeds, and air-dry.

6. Sage (Salvia officinalis):

Seed Saving:

Allow sage plants to flower and form seeds.

Harvest dried seed heads, thresh to get rid of seeds, and air-dry.

Store seeds in a cool, dry location.

7. Oregano (Origanum vulgare):

Seed Saving:

Oregano can produce seeds; permit some plants to flower.

Harvest dried seed heads, accumulate seeds, and air-dry.

Store seeds in a groovy, dry place.

8. Cilantro/Coriander (Coriandrum sativum):

Seed Saving:

Allow cilantro to bolt and produce seeds (coriander).

Harvest dried seed heads, gather seeds, and air-dry.

Store seeds in a fab, dry area.

nine. Chives (Allium schoenoprasum):

Seed Saving:

Allow chive plant life to mature and form seeds.

Harvest dried seed heads, accumulate seeds, and air-dry.

Store seeds in a groovy, dry location.

10. Dill (Anethum graveolens):

Seed Saving:

Dill produces abundant seeds; allow flora to flower.

Harvest dried seed heads, gather seeds, and air-dry.

Store seeds in a groovy, dry area.

11. Lavender (Lavandula):

Seed Saving:

Lavender is often propagated through cuttings.

Allow a few flora to flower and shape seeds.

Harvest dried flower spikes, gather seeds, and air-dry.

12. Lemon Balm (Melissa officinalis):

Seed Saving:

Lemon balm can produce seeds; permit some plant life to flower.

Harvest dried seed heads, gather seeds, and air-dry.

Store seeds in a cool, dry region.

thirteen. Chamomile (Matricaria chamomilla):

Seed Saving:

Chamomile produces seeds in the 2nd year; permit flowering.

Harvest dried seed heads, acquire seeds, and air-dry.

Store seeds in a fab, dry vicinity.

14. Fennel (Foeniculum vulgare):

Seed Saving:

Fennel produces ok seeds; permit some vegetation to flower.

Harvest dried seed heads, collect seeds, and air-dry.

Store seeds in a cool, dry place.

15. Catnip (Nepeta cataria):

Seed Saving:

Catnip produces seeds; allow some flowers to flower.

Harvest dried seed heads, acquire seeds, and air-dry.

Store seeds in a fab, dry vicinity.

sixteen. Stevia (Stevia rebaudiana):

Seed Saving:

Stevia can produce seeds; allow some plants to flower.

Harvest dried seed heads, acquire seeds, and air-dry.

Store seeds in a groovy, dry vicinity.

17. Tarragon (Artemisia dracunculus):

Seed Saving:

Tarragon is often propagated via cuttings.

Allow a few vegetation to flower and form seeds.

Harvest dried seed heads, collect seeds, and air-dry.

18. Bay Laurel (Laurus nobilis):

Seed Saving:

Bay laurel is typically propagated through cuttings.

Consider air layering for propagation.

19. Lemongrass (Cymbopogon):

Seed Saving:

Lemongrass is typically propagated thru department.

Consider dividing mature clumps for emblem spanking new plants.

20. Cumin (Cuminum cyminum):

Seed Saving:

Cumin produces seeds in its second twelve months.

Allow some flora to flower, harvest dried seed heads, and air-dry.

Store seeds in a fab, dry vicinity.

21. Cress (Lepidium sativum):

Seed Saving:

Cress produces seeds notably brief.

Allow plant life to flower, harvest dried seed heads, and air-dry.

Store seeds in a fab, dry place.

22. Lovage (Levisticum officinale):

Seed Saving:

Lovage produces seeds in its 2d twelve months.

Allow a few plants to flower, harvest dried seed heads, and air-dry.

Store seeds in a cool, dry place.

23. Sorrel (Rumex acetosa):

Seed Saving:

Sorrel produces seeds; allow some plant life to flower.

Harvest dried seed heads, accumulate seeds, and air-dry.

Store seeds in a cool, dry location.

24. Epazote (Dysphania ambrosioides):

Seed Saving:

Epazote can produce seeds; allow some plants to flower.

Harvest dried seed heads, acquire seeds, and air-dry.

Store seeds in a cool, dry region.

25. Hyssop (Hyssopus officinalis):

Seed Saving:

Hyssop produces seeds; permit a few flowers to flower.

Harvest dried seed heads, accumulate seeds, and air-dry.

Store seeds in a groovy, dry location.

26. Angelica (Angelica archangelica):

Seed Saving:

Angelica produces seeds; permit a few plants to flower.

Harvest dried seed heads, accumulate seeds, and air-dry.

Store seeds in a groovy, dry region.

27. Savory (Satureja):

Seed Saving:

Savory produces seeds; allow some plant life to flower.

Harvest dried seed heads, accumulate seeds, and air-dry.

Store seeds in a groovy, dry area.

28. Borage (Borago officinalis):

Seed Saving:

Borage produces seeds; allow some flowers to flower.

Harvest dried seed heads, accumulate seeds, and air-dry.

Store seeds in a cool, dry location.

29. Wintergreen (Gaultheria procumbens):

Seed Saving:

Wintergreen is often propagated through cuttings.

Consider branch for propagation.

30. Chervil (Anthriscus cerefolium):

Seed Saving:

Chervil produces seeds; permit some plants to flower.

Harvest dried seed heads, accumulate seeds, and air-dry.

Store seeds in a fab, dry vicinity.

Remember to label your seeds with the herb call and the three hundred and sixty five days of series. By preserving those seeds, you could make certain a non-stop deliver of smooth herbs on your culinary and medicinal desires.

A Guide to Saving Seeds from Culinary and Medicinal Plants

Embark on a journey to create your personal sustainable apothecary and spice rack with the aid of gaining knowledge of the paintings of seed saving. This manual explores the nuances of harvesting and saving seeds from a diverse array of culinary and medicinal plants:

Culinary Plants:

1. Basil (Ocimum basilicum):

Seed Saving:

Allow basil flora to bloom and produce seeds.

Harvest dried seed heads, thresh to eliminate seeds, and air-dry.

Store in a groovy, dry area.

2. Turmeric (Curcuma longa):

Seed Saving:

Turmeric is propagated via rhizomes.

Divide rhizomes at a few level inside the growing season for emblem spanking new flowers.

three. Ginger (Zingiber officinale):

Seed Saving:

Ginger is grown from rhizomes.

Harvest mature rhizomes for propagation.

4. Cumin (Cuminum cyminum):

Seed Saving:

Cumin produces seeds in its second 3 hundred and sixty 5 days.

Allow some plants to flower, harvest dried seed heads, and air-dry.

Store seeds in a fab, dry vicinity.

five. Coriander (Coriandrum sativum):

Seed Saving:

Allow cilantro to bolt and bring seeds (coriander).

Harvest dried seed heads, accumulate seeds, and air-dry.

Store seeds in a fab, dry location.

6. Sage (Salvia officinalis):

Seed Saving:

Allow sage plants to flower and form seeds.

Harvest dried seed heads, thresh to take away seeds, and air-dry.

Store in a cool, dry vicinity.

7. Thyme (Thymus):

Seed Saving:

Thyme won't produce big seeds; preserve in thoughts department.

Allow a few flora to flower and shape seeds.

Harvest dried seed heads, gather seeds, and air-dry.

8. Lavender (Lavandula):

Seed Saving:

Lavender is frequently propagated via cuttings.

Allow a few flora to flower and shape seeds.

Harvest dried flower spikes, gather seeds, and air-dry.

9. Fennel (Foeniculum vulgare):

Seed Saving:

Fennel produces adequate seeds; permit a few plant life to flower.

Harvest dried seed heads, accumulate seeds, and air-dry.

Store seeds in a groovy, dry area.

10. Dill (Anethum graveolens):

Seed Saving:

Dill produces sufficient seeds; permit flora to flower.

Harvest dried seed heads, accumulate seeds, and air-dry.

Store seeds in a fab, dry vicinity.

11. Oregano (Origanum vulgare):

Seed Saving:

Oregano can produce seeds; allow some flora to flower.

Harvest dried seed heads, gather seeds, and air-dry.

Store seeds in a groovy, dry vicinity.

12. Mint (Mentha):

Seed Saving:

Mint has a tendency to spread thru rhizomes; seed saving is non-compulsory.

Allow some flowers to flower and shape seeds.

Harvest dried seed heads, acquire seeds, and air-dry.

thirteen. Cilantro/Coriander (Coriandrum sativum):

Seed Saving:

Allow cilantro to bolt and bring seeds (coriander).

Harvest dried seed heads, collect seeds, and air-dry.

Chapter 4: Techniques for Seed Saving and Unique Considerations

Techniques for Seed Saving:

Basic Seed Saving Steps:

Harvest at the Right Time: Collect seeds while they are mature, regularly indicated by means of way of a change in colour or at the same time as the seed heads are dry.

Dry Thoroughly: Ensure seeds are absolutely dry in advance than storage to prevent mildew.

Clean Seeds: Remove debris and chaff from seeds before storing.

Open-Pollinated Plants:

Isolation Distance: Maintain enough distance among precise kinds to prevent circulate-pollination. Use bodily boundaries or time planting to keep away from pollination overlap.

Biennial Plants:

Overwintering: Allow biennials like carrots and beets to overwinter in the floor for seed production within the second yr. Harvest seeds when they mature the subsequent season.

Perennials:

Propagation Method: Some perennials, like rhubarb or berries, are usually propagated through divisions in area of seeds.

Herbs:

Cutting Propagation: Many herbs are first-class propagated through cuttings or division in preference to seeds. For seed saving, permit a few flowers to flower, harvest seeds, and air-dry.

Flowers:

Deadheading: Encourage continuous blooming via deadheading vegetation. Allow some plants to mature for seed manufacturing.

Unique Considerations for Various Plants:

Tomatoes (Solanaceae):

Fermentation Process: Extract seeds, location in a jar with water, and permit to ferment for a few days. Clean and dry seeds after fermentation.

Lettuce (Leafy Greens):

Bolting and Seed Collection: Allow lettuce to bolt (produce a flower stalk) and collect seeds from the fluffy seed heads.

Carrots (Root Vegetables):

Overwintering: Leave some carrots inside the ground thru iciness for seed production the following 365 days. Harvest seeds from the flowering flora.

Broccoli (Crucifers):

Protect from Cross-Pollination: Use row covers to guard broccoli from skip-pollination with other cruciferous flowers.

Sunflowers (Flowers):

Air-Dry Heads: Harvest sunflower heads at the same time as seeds are mature but now not absolutely dry. Allow them to finish drying interior.

Basil (Herbs):

Flower Pinching: Pinch lower back basil plant life to encourage leaf manufacturing. Allow a few plants to flower for seed manufacturing.

Mint (Herbs):

Rhizome Division: Mint spreads via rhizomes; seed saving is elective. Divide and transplant rhizomes for logo spanking new plant life.

Chamomile (Herbs):

Second-Year Flowering: Chamomile regularly produces seeds in the 2d 12 months. Harvest dried seed heads for seed series.

Cilantro/Coriander (Herbs):

Two-in-One Harvest: Allow cilantro to bolt for coriander seed manufacturing. Harvest dried seed heads for coriander.

Rosemary (Herbs):

Cuttings: Rosemary is regularly propagated through cuttings. Allow a few vegetation to flower for seed collection if preferred.

Fennel (Herbs):

Ample Spacing: Fennel produces massive seeds; provide ok spacing to prevent crowding.

Lemon Balm (Herbs):

Flowering Plants: Allow a few lemon balm flora to flower for seed production. Harvest dried seed heads for collection.

Cumin (Herbs):

Second-Year Flowering: Cumin frequently produces seeds in the second one year. Harvest dried seed heads for series.

Calendula (Medicinal and Culinary):

Continuous Blooming: Deadhead spent plant life to inspire non-prevent blooming. Harvest dried seed heads for seed collection.

Echinacea (Medicinal):

Mature Cone Heads: Harvest echinacea seeds from mature cone heads after flowering. Air-dry for seed garage.

Saffron (Medicinal):

Corm Division: Saffron is propagated via corms. Divide corms for propagation.

Licorice (Medicinal):

Root Division: Licorice is propagated through root branch. Divide roots for propagation.

Milk Thistle (Medicinal):

Mature Seed Heads: Harvest milk thistle seeds from mature seed heads. Air-dry for seed garage.

Chapter 5: Seed Saving Guide for Apple Varieties

Apples (Malus domestica) are not pleasant a famous fruit but additionally a joy to domesticate from seeds. This comprehensive guide will walk you via the seed-saving way for ten one-of-a-type apple varieties: McIntosh, Granny Smith, Gala, Fuji, Honeycrisp, Red Delicious, Golden Delicious, Pink Lady, Braeburn, and Jonathan.

1. McIntosh:

Harvesting: Collect ripe McIntosh apples from the tree. Choose apples that have reached complete color and without problems emerge as impartial from the tree.

Processing: Cut the apple and extract the seeds from the middle. Rinse seeds to take away any fruit residue.

Storage: Air-dry the seeds thoroughly. Store in a cool, darkish area in an hermetic discipline.

2. Granny Smith:

Harvesting: Gather Granny Smith apples while virtually ripened. Look for a shiny inexperienced coloration and a crisp texture.

Processing: Remove seeds from the center and smooth them. Ensure all fruit remnants are washed away.

Storage: Air-dry seeds genuinely in advance than garage. Keep in a cool, darkish vicinity.

3. Gala:

Harvesting: Harvest Gala apples after they exhibit their function color. The pores and pores and skin need to have a reddish-orange blush.

Processing: Extract seeds, smooth, and do away with any clinging fruit flesh. Wash seeds thoroughly.

Storage: Allow seeds to air-dry. Store in a fab, dark vicinity.

four. Fuji:

Harvesting: Collect Fuji apples while they will be completely mature. Look for a mixture of yellow and red pores and skin.

Processing: Remove seeds and smooth them cautiously. Ensure no fruit remnants stay.

Storage: Air-dry seeds very well. Store in a cool, dark vicinity.

five. Honeycrisp:

Harvesting: Harvest Honeycrisp apples at top ripeness. The apple have to expose off a crisp texture and a aggregate of red and inexperienced solar sunglasses.

Processing: Extract seeds, smooth, and eliminate any closing fruit. Thoroughly wash the seeds.

Storage: Air-dry seeds absolutely. Store in a fab, dark area.

6. Red Delicious:

Harvesting: Collect Red Delicious apples whilst they are completely red and corporation. Choose apples which can be free from blemishes.

Processing: Extract seeds, easy, and do away with any pulp. Rinse seeds thoroughly.

Storage: Allow seeds to air-dry. Store in a fab, darkish location.

7. Golden Delicious:

Harvesting: Harvest Golden Delicious apples at the same time as surely yellow and barely smooth. Ensure the apples have a candy aroma.

Processing: Extract seeds, clean, and take away any residue. Wash seeds thoroughly.

Storage: Air-dry seeds honestly. Store in a cool, dark place.

8. Pink Lady:

Harvesting: Gather Pink Lady apples while sincerely ripe. Look for apples with a pinkish-crimson skin.

Processing: Remove seeds from the center, clean, and wash them. Ensure no fruit remnants live.

Storage: Allow seeds to air-dry. Store in a groovy, dark place.

nine. Braeburn:

Harvesting: Harvest Braeburn apples while in reality colored. Look for a pink-orange blush on a yellow-green records.

Processing: Extract seeds, smooth, and take away any clinging fruit. Rinse seeds very well.

Storage: Air-dry seeds completely. Store in a fab, dark location.

10. Jonathan:

Harvesting: Collect Jonathan apples at the identical time as they're genuinely crimson and crisp. Ensure apples are free from ailment or pests.

Processing: Remove seeds, clean, and wash very well. Eliminate any fruit residue.

Storage: Allow seeds to air-dry. Store in a cool, dark place.

General Tips for Apple Seed Saving:

Maturity Matters: Harvest apples even as they may be simply mature for possible seeds.

Cleaning Process: Thoroughly easy seeds to take away any fruit residue.

Air-Drying: Allow seeds to air-dry completely earlier than storage.

Storage Conditions: Store seeds in hermetic bins in a cool, dark area.

Stratification (Optional): Some apple seeds may additionally moreover benefit from cold stratification in advance than planting.

Labeling: Clearly label packing containers with the apple range and the date of seed collection.

By following those steps, you can efficiently keep seeds from diverse apple kinds, permitting you to develop your favorite apples in your lawn.

Seed Saving Guide for Pear Varieties

Pears (Pyrus) are exceptional end result, and saving their seeds allows you to broaden those delicious kinds for your very own garden. This guide will take you thru the seed-saving technique for ten excellent pear sorts: Bartlett, Anjou, Bosc, Comice, Asian Pear, Forelle, Seckel, Starkrimson, Concorde, and Abate Fetel.

1. Bartlett:

Harvesting: Collect Bartlett pears when they have reached entire ripeness. Choose pears that have a yellow color and yield barely to strain.

Processing: Cut the pear and extract the seeds from the center. Rinse seeds very well to get rid of any ultimate fruit flesh.

Storage: Air-dry the seeds absolutely. Store in a cool, dark area in an hermetic discipline.

2. Anjou:

Harvesting: Harvest Anjou pears while they may be mature however notwithstanding the reality that employer. Look for a inexperienced or yellow coloration, counting on the variety.

Processing: Remove seeds from the middle and clean them. Wash seeds thoroughly to put off any fruit residue.

Storage: Allow seeds to air-dry simply. Store in a fab, dark area.

three. Bosc:

Harvesting: Gather Bosc pears after they have a brownish shade and are barely business enterprise. Avoid equipped till they come to be overly slight.

Processing: Extract seeds, smooth, and eliminate any clinging fruit. Rinse seeds very well.

Storage: Air-dry seeds without a doubt. Store in a fab, dark place.

four. Comice:

Harvesting: Harvest Comice pears at the same time as they'll be surely ripe and function a yellow-inexperienced color. Choose pears which may be fragrant and yield slightly to strain.

Processing: Remove seeds from the center and easy them. Wash seeds very well to dispose of any fruit remnants.

Storage: Allow seeds to air-dry surely. Store in a groovy, dark region.

5. Asian Pear:

Harvesting: Collect Asian pears even as they're honestly mature. Look for a crisp texture and a yellow or brownish pores and pores and skin colour.

Processing: Extract seeds, smooth, and remove any clinging fruit. Rinse seeds thoroughly.

Storage: Air-dry seeds genuinely. Store in a cool, dark place.

6. Forelle:

Harvesting: Harvest Forelle pears while they'll be absolutely ripe. Look for a yellow-inexperienced coloration with purple freckles.

Processing: Remove seeds from the middle, smooth, and wash them. Ensure no fruit remnants stay.

Storage: Allow seeds to air-dry completely. Store in a fab, darkish vicinity.

7. Seckel:

Harvesting: Gather Seckel pears at the same time as they may be surely mature. Choose pears with a reddish-brown shade.

Processing: Extract seeds, easy, and do away with any final fruit. Rinse seeds thoroughly.

Storage: Air-dry seeds virtually. Store in a groovy, darkish vicinity.

eight. Starkrimson:

Harvesting: Harvest Starkrimson pears at the same time as sincerely ripened. Choose pears with a deep purple color.

Processing: Remove seeds from the center and smooth them. Wash seeds thoroughly.

Storage: Allow seeds to air-dry completely. Store in a groovy, darkish region.

nine. Concorde:

Harvesting: Collect Concorde pears while they're mature but even though corporation. Look for a green colour with a moderate yellow blush.

Processing: Extract seeds, clean, and eliminate any clinging fruit. Rinse seeds thoroughly.

Storage: Air-dry seeds truly. Store in a groovy, darkish vicinity.

10. Abate Fetel:

Harvesting: Harvest Abate Fetel pears at the same time as absolutely ripe. Look for a yellow color with a pink blush.

Processing: Remove seeds from the middle, easy, and wash them. Ensure no fruit remnants remain.

Storage: Allow seeds to air-dry truly. Store in a cool, darkish place.

General Tips for Pear Seed Saving:

Maturity Matters: Harvest pears at the same time as they are completely mature for possible seeds.

Cleaning Process: Thoroughly smooth seeds to do away with any fruit residue.

Air-Drying: Allow seeds to air-dry completely earlier than garage.

Storage Conditions: Store seeds in hermetic packing containers in a groovy, darkish area.

Stratification (Optional): Some pear seeds may also moreover additionally gain from bloodless stratification earlier than planting.

Labeling: Clearly label packing containers with the pear range and the date of seed series.

By following those steps, you can effectively save seeds from numerous pear kinds, allowing you to increase those first-rate stop bring about your lawn. Happy seed saving!

Chapter 6: Seed Saving Guide for Stone Fruits

Stone stop result, which includes peaches, plums, and cherries, are not first rate delicious however also provide the possibility for home gardeners to preserve and increase seeds. This complete manual will walk you thru the seed-saving approach for ten specific stone fruit types: Peach, Nectarine, Apricot, Plum, Cherry (Sweet), Cherry (Sour), Black Plum, White Peach, Yellow Plum, and Rainier Cherry.

1. Peach:

Harvesting: Collect peaches whilst they may be fully ripe and feature a colorful coloration. Choose peaches with a mild yield to strain.

Processing: Cut the peach, extract seeds from the pit, and smooth them. Rinse seeds thoroughly to eliminate any clinging fruit flesh.

Storage: Air-dry seeds certainly. Store in a fab, dark vicinity.

2. Nectarine:

Harvesting: Harvest nectarines at the same time as completely ripe and characteristic a smooth pores and pores and skin. Choose nectarines with a candy aroma.

Processing: Remove seeds from the pit and clean them. Wash seeds thoroughly.

Storage: Allow seeds to air-dry truely. Store in a cool, dark area.

3. Apricot:

Harvesting: Collect apricots whilst they're completely ripe and feature a wealthy orange color. Choose apricots that yield slightly to stress.

Processing: Extract seeds from the pit, smooth, and wash them. Ensure no fruit remnants live.

Storage: Air-dry seeds surely. Store in a fab, dark location.

4. Plum:

Harvesting: Harvest plums on the equal time as definitely ripe and have a deep shade. Choose plums with a slight softness.

Processing: Remove seeds from the pit, smooth, and wash them. Rinse seeds very well.

Storage: Allow seeds to air-dry without a doubt. Store in a groovy, darkish place.

5. Cherry (Sweet):

Harvesting: Harvest sweet cherries when surely ripe and have a deep purple shade. Choose cherries with a organisation texture.

Processing: Extract seeds from the fruit, easy, and wash them. Ensure no fruit remnants live.

Storage: Air-dry seeds completely. Store in a groovy, darkish area.

6. Cherry (Sour):

Harvesting: Harvest sour cherries on the equal time as they're completely mature and feature a terrific crimson shade. Choose cherries with a tangy flavor.

Processing: Remove seeds from the fruit, smooth, and wash them. Rinse seeds thoroughly.

Storage: Allow seeds to air-dry virtually. Store in a groovy, darkish location.

7. Black Plum:

Harvesting: Harvest black plums at the same time as sincerely ripe and feature a darkish red to black color. Choose plums with a gentle texture.

Processing: Extract seeds from the pit, clean, and wash them. Ensure no fruit remnants live.

Storage: Air-dry seeds absolutely. Store in a fab, darkish location.

eight. White Peach:

Harvesting: Harvest white peaches whilst certainly ripe and feature a creamy-white colour. Choose peaches with a moderate yield to stress.

Processing: Remove seeds from the pit, easy, and wash them. Rinse seeds thoroughly.

Storage: Allow seeds to air-dry absolutely. Store in a fab, dark area.

9. Yellow Plum:

Harvesting: Harvest yellow plums whilst truely ripe and feature a golden-yellow shade. Choose plums with a barely business enterprise texture.

Processing: Extract seeds from the pit, clean, and wash them. Ensure no fruit remnants stay.

Storage: Air-dry seeds completely. Store in a groovy, dark place.

10. Rainier Cherry:

Harvesting: Harvest Rainier cherries on the identical time as clearly ripe and characteristic a yellow and purple blush. Choose cherries with a sweet and creamy taste.

Processing: Remove seeds from the fruit, smooth, and wash them. Rinse seeds thoroughly.

Storage: Allow seeds to air-dry surely. Store in a cool, dark region.

General Tips for Stone Fruit Seed Saving:

Maturity Matters: Harvest fruits while fully mature for possible seeds.

Cleaning Process: Thoroughly clean seeds to remove any fruit residue.

Air-Drying: Allow seeds to air-dry clearly earlier than storage.

Storage Conditions: Store seeds in hermetic bins in a fab, dark vicinity.

Labeling: Clearly label packing containers with the fruit variety and the date of seed collection.

By following the ones steps, you may efficiently shop seeds from diverse stone fruit types, allowing you to increase your preferred peaches, plums, and cherries on your garden. Happy seed saving!

Seed Saving Guide for Nuts and Seeds from Trees: Acorns (Oak Trees)

Nuts and seeds from timber, together with acorns from okaytrees, are treasured for propagating the ones majestic woody plants. This top notch manual will stroll you thru the seed-saving device for ten considered one of a kind alrighttree kinds: Northern Red Oak, White Oak, Bur Oak, Pin Oak, Scarlet Oak, Shumard Oak, Swamp Chestnut Oak, Willow Oak, Water Oak, and Post Oak.

1. Northern Red Oak:

Harvesting: Collect acorns from Northern Red Oak whilst they'll be absolutely mature. Choose acorns with a wealthy brown color and a enterprise shell.

Processing: Remove acorns from their caps and easy them. Discard any acorns with holes or symptoms and signs of pests.

Storage: Allow acorns to air-dry definitely. Store in a groovy, dry area.

2. White Oak:

Harvesting: Harvest acorns from White Oak while they will be in fact ripened. Look for acorns with a mild brown coloration and a slightly rounded cap.

Processing: Separate acorns from their caps and easy them thoroughly. Discard any acorns displaying signs and symptoms of sickness or damage.

Storage: Air-dry acorns completely. Store in a cool, dry place.

three. Bur Oak:

Harvesting: Collect acorns from Bur Oak at the same time as they are completely mature. Choose acorns with a huge duration and a slight brown colour.

Processing: Remove acorns from their caps and smooth them. Discard any acorns with cracks or holes.

Storage: Allow acorns to air-dry absolutely. Store in a fab, dry area.

four. Pin Oak:

Harvesting: Harvest acorns from Pin Oak while they will be completely ripe. Choose acorns with a characteristic pin-like shape.

Processing: Separate acorns from their caps and clean them. Discard any acorns with broken or deformed shells.

Storage: Air-dry acorns simply. Store in a cool, dry vicinity.

5. Scarlet Oak:

Harvesting: Collect acorns from Scarlet Oak after they have reached whole maturity. Look for acorns with a deep purple-brown color.

Processing: Remove acorns from their caps and smooth them very well. Discard any acorns showing symptoms of insect infestation.

Storage: Allow acorns to air-dry completely. Store in a fab, dry area.

6. Shumard Oak:

Harvesting: Harvest acorns from Shumard Oak while they will be clearly mature. Choose acorns with a reddish-brown shade and a company shell.

Processing: Separate acorns from their caps and smooth them. Discard any acorns with seen harm.

Storage: Air-dry acorns in fact. Store in a groovy, dry location.

7. Swamp Chestnut Oak:

Harvesting: Collect acorns from Swamp Chestnut Oak at the equal time as they're completely ripe. Look for acorns with a chestnut-like appearance.

Processing: Remove acorns from their caps and clean them. Discard any acorns with mold or discoloration.

Storage: Allow acorns to air-dry virtually. Store in a groovy, dry region.

8. Willow Oak:

Harvesting: Harvest acorns from Willow Oak at the same time as they may be fully mature. Choose acorns with a slim form and a moderate brown colour.

Processing: Separate acorns from their caps and clean them very well. Discard any acorns with seen harm.

Storage: Air-dry acorns definitely. Store in a groovy, dry location.

Chapter 7: Seed Saving Guide for Chestnuts

Chestnuts aren't simplest scrumptious nuts however moreover offer the opportunity for home gardeners to keep and grow their private chestnut timber. This guide will walk you through the seed-saving method for ten precise chestnut kinds: American Chestnut, Chinese Chestnut, Japanese Chestnut, European Chestnut, Korean Chestnut, Allegheny Chinkapin, Henry's Chestnut, Sawtooth Oak, Sweet Chestnut, and Chestnut Oak.

1. American Chestnut:

Harvesting: Collect American chestnuts when they fall to the ground, normally in late summer season or early fall. Choose nuts with a corporation shell and no signs and signs and symptoms of harm.

Processing: Remove the outer husk, clean the nuts, and air-dry them very well.

Storage: Store American chestnuts in a cool, dry place.

2. Chinese Chestnut:

Harvesting: Harvest Chinese chestnuts after they fall from the tree in overdue summer time or early fall. Choose nuts with a easy, intact husk.

Processing: Remove the husk, smooth the nuts, and air-dry them very well.

Storage: Store Chinese chestnuts in a groovy, dry place.

3. Japanese Chestnut:

Harvesting: Collect Japanese chestnuts after they fall from the tree. Choose nuts with a smooth, spiky husk.

Processing: Remove the husk, easy the nuts, and air-dry them very well.

Storage: Store Japanese chestnuts in a cool, dry location.

four. European Chestnut:

Harvesting: Harvest European chestnuts after they fall from the tree. Choose nuts with a organisation, intact husk.

Processing: Remove the husk, clean the nuts, and air-dry them very well.

Storage: Store European chestnuts in a fab, dry region.

5. Korean Chestnut:

Harvesting: Collect Korean chestnuts when they fall from the tree. Choose nuts with a easy, spiky husk.

Processing: Remove the husk, easy the nuts, and air-dry them thoroughly.

Storage: Store Korean chestnuts in a cool, dry place.

6. Allegheny Chinkapin:

Harvesting: Harvest Allegheny chinkapins after they fall from the tree. Choose nuts with a clean, spiky husk.

Processing: Remove the husk, clean the nuts, and air-dry them very well.

Storage: Store Allegheny chinkapins in a cool, dry place.

7. Henry's Chestnut:

Harvesting: Collect Henry's chestnuts once they fall from the tree. Choose nuts with a easy, intact husk.

Processing: Remove the husk, easy the nuts, and air-dry them very well.

Storage: Store Henry's chestnuts in a fab, dry vicinity.

eight. Sawtooth Oak:

Harvesting: Harvest Sawtooth acorns after they fall from the tree. Choose nuts with a smooth, spiky husk.

Processing: Remove the husk, easy the nuts, and air-dry them thoroughly.

Storage: Store Sawtooth acorns in a groovy, dry vicinity.

nine. Sweet Chestnut:

Harvesting: Harvest candy chestnuts when they fall from the tree. Choose nuts with a easy, intact husk.

Processing: Remove the husk, smooth the nuts, and air-dry them very well.

Storage: Store candy chestnuts in a groovy, dry vicinity.

10. Chestnut Oak:

Harvesting: Collect Chestnut all rightacorns when they fall from the tree. Choose nuts with a easy, spiky husk.

Processing: Remove the husk, clean the nuts, and air-dry them very well.

Storage: Store Chestnut okayacorns in a groovy, dry vicinity.

General Tips for Chestnut Seed Saving:

Harvest Timing: Collect chestnuts once they glaringly fall or whilst the husks begin to break up.

Husk Removal: Remove husks promptly to save you mildew and make sure seed viability.

Air-Drying: Allow nuts to air-dry definitely in advance than garage.

Storage Conditions: Store chestnuts in airtight bins in a cool, dry place.

Labeling: Clearly label containers with the chestnut range and the date of nut series.

By following the ones steps, you could efficiently save seeds from numerous chestnut sorts, allowing you to grow your very own chestnut bushes and revel in the flavorful nuts they produce. Happy seed saving!

Seed Saving Guide for Pine Nuts

Pine nuts, harvested from various pine tree species, are not most effective delicious but additionally offer the opportunity for domestic gardeners to save and increase their very very personal pine timber. This manual will walk you via the seed-saving approach for ten exceptional pine nut kinds: Ponderosa Pine, Pinon Pine, Stone Pine, Korean Pine, Singleleaf Pinyon, Lacebark Pine, Mexican Pinyon, Chilgoza Pine, Jeffrey Pine, and Sugar Pine.

1. Ponderosa Pine:

Harvesting: Collect ponderosa pine cones when they flip brown and open definitely. Choose cones with tightly packed seeds.

Processing: Extract seeds by tapping the cones gently to release them. Clean the seeds and air-dry them very well.

Storage: Store ponderosa pine seeds in a fab, dry region.

2. Pinon Pine:

Harvesting: Harvest pinon pine cones once they turn brown and open sincerely. Choose cones with plump, well-filled seeds.

Processing: Extract seeds with the aid of way of tapping the cones lightly to launch them. Clean the seeds and air-dry them very well.

Storage: Store pinon pine seeds in a fab, dry location.

3. Stone Pine:

Harvesting: Collect stone pine cones once they begin to open and seeds are seen. Choose cones with completely advanced seeds.

Processing: Extract seeds through tapping the cones lightly to release them. Clean the seeds and air-dry them thoroughly.

Storage: Store stone pine seeds in a groovy, dry vicinity.

four. Korean Pine:

Harvesting: Harvest Korean pine cones when they flip brown and open honestly. Choose cones with properly-stuffed, mature seeds.

Processing: Extract seeds by means of tapping the cones gently to release them. Clean the seeds and air-dry them thoroughly.

Storage: Store Korean pine seeds in a cool, dry place.

5. Singleleaf Pinyon:

Harvesting: Collect singleleaf pinyon cones once they flip brown and open certainly. Choose cones with plump, nicely-crammed seeds.

Processing: Extract seeds by using way of tapping the cones lightly to launch them. Clean the seeds and air-dry them thoroughly.

Storage: Store singleleaf pinyon seeds in a cool, dry location.

6. Lacebark Pine:

Harvesting: Harvest lacebark pine cones after they turn brown and open certainly. Choose cones with nicely-superior seeds.

Processing: Extract seeds with the useful aid of tapping the cones lightly to launch them. Clean the seeds and air-dry them very well.

Storage: Store lacebark pine seeds in a groovy, dry region.

7. Mexican Pinyon:

Harvesting: Collect Mexican pinyon cones once they flip brown and open virtually. Choose cones with plump, nicely-crammed seeds.

Processing: Extract seeds thru tapping the cones lightly to launch them. Clean the seeds and air-dry them very well.

Storage: Store Mexican pinyon seeds in a fab, dry area.

8. Chilgoza Pine:

Harvesting: Harvest chilgoza pine cones when they flip brown and open certainly. Choose cones with absolutely evolved seeds.

Processing: Extract seeds by way of tapping the cones lightly to launch them. Clean the seeds and air-dry them thoroughly.

Storage: Store chilgoza pine seeds in a groovy, dry area.

9. Jeffrey Pine:

Harvesting: Collect Jeffrey pine cones after they turn brown and open simply. Choose cones with nicely-superior seeds.

Processing: Extract seeds thru tapping the cones lightly to release them. Clean the seeds and air-dry them very well.

Storage: Store Jeffrey pine seeds in a groovy, dry place.

10. Sugar Pine:

Harvesting: Harvest sugar pine cones when they flip brown and open truely. Choose cones with nicely-filled, mature seeds.

Processing: Extract seeds through tapping the cones gently to launch them. Clean the seeds and air-dry them thoroughly.

Storage: Store sugar pine seeds in a cool, dry region.

General Tips for Pine Nut Seed Saving:

Timing is Crucial: Harvest pine cones once they glaringly open, revealing mature seeds.

Gentle Extraction: Tap cones gently to launch seeds with out damaging them.

Thorough Drying: Ensure seeds are in reality dry earlier than storage to prevent mold.

Storage Conditions: Store pine seeds in hermetic bins in a fab, dry vicinity.

Labeling: Clearly label boxes with the pine nut range and the date of seed series.

By following those steps, you may correctly preserve seeds from various pine nut kinds, allowing you to increase your very very own pine wood and revel in the first-rate nuts they produce. Happy seed saving!

Seed Saving Guide for Almonds

Almonds, with their scrumptious taste and versatility, may be grown from seeds, offering an opportunity for domestic gardeners to enjoy their private almond harvest. This guide will walk you through the seed-saving technique for ten specific almond types: Sweet Almond, Bitter Almond, Marcona Almond, Carmel Almond, Nonpareil Almond, Sonora Almond, Ne Plus Ultra Almond, Fritz Almond, Mission Almond, and Padre Almond.

Chapter 8: Avocado Seeds

Avocado bushes are stated for his or her creamy, nutritious end result, and developing them from seeds is a profitable agency. This guide will stroll you through the seed-saving approach for ten special avocado types: Hass Avocado, Fuerte Avocado, Reed Avocado, Pinkerton Avocado, 1st baron beaverbrook Avocado, Gwen Avocado, Lamb Hass Avocado, Zutano Avocado, Puebla Avocado, and Wurtz Avocado.

1. Hass Avocado:

Harvesting: Harvest Hass avocados once they have a darkish, pebbly pores and pores and skin and yield to gentle stress. Choose wholesome avocados without a signs and symptoms of rot or sickness.

Processing: Scoop out the seed from the avocado flesh. Clean the seed very well, casting off any closing flesh.

Storage: Store Hass avocado seeds in a fab, dry location.

2. Fuerte Avocado:

Harvesting: Harvest Fuerte avocados whilst they're even though barely inexperienced and yield to slight pressure. Choose avocados that are unfastened from blemishes or harm.

Processing: Remove the seed from the flesh. Clean the seed and air-dry it very well.

Storage: Store Fuerte avocado seeds in a groovy, dry area.

three. Reed Avocado:

Harvesting: Harvest Reed avocados once they have a easy, inexperienced pores and pores and skin and yield to slight strain. Choose avocados which might be plump and unfastened from clean spots.

Processing: Separate the seed from the flesh. Clean the seed and air-dry it very well.

Storage: Store Reed avocado seeds in a groovy, dry area.

four. Pinkerton Avocado:

Harvesting: Harvest Pinkerton avocados after they have a pear-like shape and yield to slight pressure. Choose avocados which may be loose from bruises or discoloration.

Processing: Remove the seed from the flesh. Clean the seed and air-dry it thoroughly.

Storage: Store Pinkerton avocado seeds in a fab, dry vicinity.

five. 1st Baron 1st Viscount St. Albans Avocado:

Harvesting: Harvest Beaverbrook avocados after they have a smooth, inexperienced pores and skin and yield to slight pressure. Choose avocados which may be loose from blemishes or damage.

Processing: Scoop out the seed from the avocado flesh. Clean the seed very well, getting rid of any very last flesh.

Storage: Store 1st Baron Beaverbrook avocado seeds in a groovy, dry vicinity.

6. Gwen Avocado:

Harvesting: Harvest Gwen avocados after they have a small to medium length and yield to mild stress. Choose avocados which can be unfastened from blemishes or smooth spots.

Processing: Remove the seed from the flesh. Clean the seed and air-dry it thoroughly.

Storage: Store Gwen avocado seeds in a groovy, dry region.

7. Lamb Hass Avocado:

Harvesting: Harvest Lamb Hass avocados once they have a darkish, pebbly pores and skin and yield to mild stress. Choose wholesome avocados without a signs and symptoms of rot or illness.

Processing: Scoop out the seed from the avocado flesh. Clean the seed thoroughly, removing any very last flesh.

Storage: Store Lamb Hass avocado seeds in a fab, dry vicinity.

8. Zutano Avocado:

Harvesting: Harvest Zutano avocados after they have a pear-like shape and yield to mild stress. Choose avocados which might be unfastened from bruises or discoloration.

Processing: Remove the seed from the flesh. Clean the seed and air-dry it thoroughly.

Storage: Store Zutano avocado seeds in a cool, dry location.

nine. Puebla Avocado:

Harvesting: Harvest Puebla avocados once they have a clean, green pores and skin and yield to slight strain. Choose avocados which may be plump and loose from mild spots.

Processing: Separate the seed from the flesh. Clean the seed and air-dry it thoroughly.

Storage: Store Puebla avocado seeds in a fab, dry area.

10. Wurtz Avocado:

Harvesting: Harvest Wurtz avocados once they have a small to medium size and yield to mild pressure. Choose avocados which might be unfastened from blemishes or clean spots.

Processing: Remove the seed from the flesh. Clean the seed and air-dry it thoroughly.

Storage: Store Wurtz avocado seeds in a groovy, dry area.

General Tips for Avocado Seed Saving:

Harvest Maturity: Harvest avocados whilst they will be mature and yield to slight strain.

Gentle Processing: Carefully do away with the seed from the flesh to avoid harm.

Thorough Cleaning: Clean the seed very well, removing any final flesh.

Air-Drying: Allow avocado seeds to air-dry completely earlier than storage.

Storage Conditions: Store avocado seeds in hermetic boxes in a cool, dry place.

Labeling: Clearly label boxes with the avocado range and the date of seed collection.

By following those steps, you may efficiently keep seeds from severa avocado kinds, permitting you to grow your non-public avocado timber and experience the rich, buttery end result they produce. Happy seed saving!

Chapter 9: Various Fruit, Tree, and Shrub Seeds

Growing fruit, bushes, and shrubs from seeds can be a fulfilling and profitable revel in. This complete manual will walk you via the seed-saving approach for a severa range of end result, timber, and shrubs.

These embody Lemon, Orange, Lime, Grapefruit, Mango, Papaya, Pineapple, Banana, Coconut, Olive, Fig, Mulberry, Kiwi, Persimmon, Passion Fruit, Guava, Dragon Fruit, Pomegranate, Cranberry, Blueberry, Raspberry, Blackberry, Strawberry, Gooseberry, Elderberry, Black Currant, Red Currant, White Currant, Grape, Kiwi Berry, Apricot Vine, Plum Vine, Cherry Vine, Grape Vine, Olive Tree, Citrus Tree (Generic), Peach Tree, Nectarine Tree, Avocado Tree, Banana Plant, Papaya Tree, Mango Tree, Coconut Palm, Pomegranate Bush, Fig Tree, Mulberry Tree, Persimmon Tree, Passion Fruit Vine, Guava Tree, Dragon Fruit Cactus, Walnut Tree, Chestnut Tree, Pecan Tree, Hazelnut Bush, Macadamia Nut Tree, Pistachio Tree,

Cashew Tree, Almond Tree, Olive Tree, and Pine Tree.

1. Citrus Fruits (Lemon, Orange, Lime, Grapefruit):

Harvesting: Harvest citrus quit stop result whilst they're absolutely ripened at the tree. Choose forestall give up end result which may be colourful in colour and function a aromatic aroma.

Processing: Extract seeds from the fruit. Rinse seeds thoroughly to get rid of any residual pulp.

Storage: Air-dry seeds surely earlier than storing in a groovy, dry region.

2. Tropical Fruits (Mango, Papaya, Pineapple, Banana, Coconut):

Harvesting: Harvest tropical fruits once they obtain maturity. Choose culmination with steady color and no signs and signs and symptoms of harm.

Processing: Extract seeds from the fruit. Clean seeds and air-dry very well.

Storage: Store tropical fruit seeds in a groovy, dry place.

3. Olive:

Harvesting: Harvest olives after they have reached complete length and colour. Choose olives with out blemishes or harm.

Processing: Remove seeds from the olive. Soak seeds in water to cast off any residual flesh.

Storage: Air-dry seeds actually earlier than storing in a groovy, dry area.

four. Fig:

Harvesting: Harvest figs even as they'll be simply ripe and feature a gentle texture. Choose figs which can be plump and loose from mildew.

Processing: Extract seeds from the fig. Rinse seeds very well and air-dry.

Storage: Store fig seeds in a cool, dry place.

5. Berries (Cranberry, Blueberry, Raspberry, Blackberry, Strawberry, Gooseberry, Elderberry, Black Currant, Red Currant, White Currant):

Harvesting: Harvest berries while they may be sincerely ripe and effects come off the plant. Select plump, corporation berries with out signs and symptoms and signs and symptoms of mildew.

Processing: Extract seeds from the berries. Rinse seeds very well and air-dry.

Storage: Store berry seeds in a cool, dry region.

6. Grape and Kiwi Berry:

Harvesting: Harvest grapes and kiwi berries while they will be virtually ripened at the vine. Choose grapes which are plump and feature a sweet aroma.

Processing: Extract seeds from the grapes or kiwi berries. Rinse seeds very well and air-dry.

Storage: Store grape and kiwi berry seeds in a fab, dry vicinity.

7. Stone Fruits (Apricot Vine, Plum Vine, Cherry Vine):

Harvesting: Harvest stone culmination while they may be certainly ripened on the tree. Choose fruits with colorful coloration and a sweet aroma.

Processing: Extract seeds from the stone culmination. Rinse seeds very well and air-dry.

Storage: Store stone fruit seeds in a fab, dry region.

eight. Nut Trees (Walnut, Chestnut, Pecan, Hazelnut, Macadamia Nut, Pistachio, Cashew, Almond):

Harvesting: Harvest nuts even as the outer husks split, revealing the inner shell. Choose nuts which may be intact and unfastened from mold or pests.

Processing: Crack open the outer shell to extract the nut. Rinse nuts very well and air-dry.

Storage: Store nuts in a cool, dry area.

nine. Pine Tree:

Harvesting: Harvest pine cones even as they will be absolutely mature. Choose pine cones which is probably open and feature released their seeds.

Processing: Extract seeds from the pine cones. Rinse seeds very well and air-dry.

Storage: Store pine tree seeds in a groovy, dry vicinity.

Chapter 10: A Comprehensive Guide for Home Gardeners

As we delve into the costly nation-states of home gardening, there lies an problematic dance amongst vegetation, fauna, and the environment-a dance that transcends the bounds of our outdoor and extends to the extra surroundings. In this comprehensive manual, we find out the profound dating amongst domestic gardeners and biodiversity, emphasizing the pivotal function of environmental conservation via the art work and technological expertise of seed saving.

1. Home Gardeners and Biodiversity:

a. Importance of Biodiversity in Gardens:

Biodiversity in home gardens is not certainly a chic preference; it's a key cause force of surroundings fitness. Diverse plant species create a haven for a myriad of life office work, from bugs to birds, fostering a harmonious stability inside the microcosm of your lawn.

Ecosystem Stability: A numerous variety of flowers attracts various bugs, birds, and beneficial microorganisms. This range contributes to the steadiness and resilience of the lawn's ecosystem.

Resilience to Pests and Diseases: Biodiversity acts as a natural safety mechanism. Gardens with a wealthy tapestry of vegetation are much less vulnerable to pest infestations and sickness outbreaks due to the intricacies of a balanced environment.

b. Creating Micro-Habitats:

Plant Selection: The first step inside the course of biodiversity is considerate plant choice. Choose vegetation that assist unique pollinators-bees, butterflies, and hummingbirds-growing a dynamic and vibrant garden.

Water Features: Integrate small ponds or birdbaths into your garden layout. Water functions lure amphibians and birds, reworking your lawn into a thriving micro-habitat.

2. Environmental Conservation thru Seed Saving:

a. Preserving Native Plant Varieties:

Seed saving is a workout that transcends the boundaries of the lawn, contributing appreciably to environmental conservation efforts.

Seed Banks: Participate in or help community seed banks centered on keeping native and heirloom plant types. These repositories act as guardians of biodiversity, ensuring the survival of plants uniquely adapted to particular areas.

Adaptation to Climate Change: Saving seeds from locally tailored vegetation is a proactive diploma toward weather alternate. These seeds supply the genetic information critical for flora to comply and adapt to moving climatic situations.

b. Sustainable Practices:

The ethos of seed saving aligns seamlessly with sustainable gardening practices. By embracing sustainability, domestic gardeners make contributions to the broader purpose of environmental conservation.

Organic Gardening: Reduce the use of risky chemical materials and pesticides. Embrace natural gardening practices that nurture the soil and create a extra wholesome, more numerous environment.

Companion Planting: Harness the strength of partner planting. Intermingle plants strategically to enhance biodiversity, developing alliances that deter pests and promote mutual boom.

3. The Role of Home Gardeners in Conservation:

a. Citizen Science Initiatives:

The effect of domestic gardeners extends beyond the lawn fence. Engaging in citizen era initiatives empowers people to make a contribution treasured data for broader conservation efforts.

Monitoring Biodiversity: Participate in citizen technological expertise packages centered on monitoring plant and animal species for your vicinity. Your observations grow to be important statistics points for researchers analyzing network biodiversity.

Data Collection: By contributing to statistics series efforts, home gardeners turn out to be vital partners in clinical research. This records aids in expertise trends, figuring out threats, and formulating conservation techniques.

Chapter 11: Troubleshooting And Common Challenges

Embarking on the adventure of seed saving and gardening is a profitable mission, but it comes with its proportion of stressful conditions. As you domesticate your green haven, encountering limitations is inevitable. This whole guide delves into troubleshooting the common disturbing situations faced through using seed savers and gardeners, offering insightful solutions to make sure your gardening enjoy remains colourful and fruitful.

1. Addressing Issues in Seed Saving:

a. Seed Viability and Germination:

Challenge: Low seed viability or bad germination rates can be disheartening.

Solution:

Proper Storage: Ensure seeds are saved in cool, dry conditions. Use airtight containers to save you moisture and maintain them in a darkish area.

Regular Testing: Periodically test seed viability thru assignment germination exams. This allows discover capability problems before planting.

b. Cross-Pollination:

Challenge: Unintended go-pollination can compromise the purity of seeds, specifically in open-pollinated flora.

Solution:

Isolation Techniques: Separate remarkable kinds to save you skip-pollination. Use bodily boundaries like nets or time planting to stagger flowering durations.

Hand Pollination: Consider hand-pollinating plant life if isolation is hard. This gives you manipulate over the pollination technique.

c. Disease Management:

Challenge: Diseases can impact the fitness of your flora and the viability of seeds.

Solution:

Healthy Practices: Promote ordinary plant fitness via proper watering practices, proper spacing, and nutrient-wealthy soil.

Isolate Affected Plants: If a plant indicates signs and symptoms and signs and symptoms of illness, isolate it to save you the unfold to special vegetation.

d. Insect Infestations:

Challenge: Insects, mainly seed-ingesting pests, can pose a risk to the seed-saving manner.

Solution:

Companion Planting: Cultivate associate flora that repel not unusual pests, growing a herbal protection.

Natural Predators: Attract useful insects like ladybugs and predatory wasps that prey on dangerous pests.

2. Solutions to Common Gardening Challenges:

a. Soil Quality:

Challenge: Poor soil exceptional can prevent plant boom and development.

Solution:

Soil Testing: Assess soil composition via testing. Amend the soil with natural remember, compost, or specific nutrients based totally on take a look at results.

Mulching: Mulch permits keep moisture, regulates soil temperature, and adds natural rely over time.

b. Watering Issues:

Challenge: Inconsistent watering or overwatering can cause plant stress.

Solution:

Consistent Watering: Establish a regular watering schedule, specifically within the course of essential boom tiers.

Mulching: Mulch spherical flowers to maintain soil moisture and reduce the frequency of watering.

c. Environmental Factors:

Challenge: Unfavorable climate situations, which include immoderate temperatures or unexpected frosts, can effect plant fitness.

Solution:

Seasonal Planning: Choose plant types tailor-made in your nearby climate. Plan planting times to keep away from frost or severe warmth.

Protective Measures: Use row covers or cloths to defend plant life from unfavourable climate conditions.

d. Overcrowding:

Challenge: Planting too carefully can bring about overcrowding, affecting air flow and nutrient availability.

Solution:

Proper Spacing: Follow endorsed spacing hints for each plant type.

Thinning: Regularly thin out seedlings to hold most alluring spacing as flora enlarge.

Navigating the hard panorama of seed saving and gardening calls for resilience and versatility. By statistics and addressing not unusual annoying conditions, you empower yourself to create a thriving garden and effectively preserve seeds for destiny plantings.

Remember that every assignment is an opportunity to research and refine your gardening skills. As you embark on this inexperienced journey, embody the rhythm of nature, have a superb time the victories, and take a look at from the worrying conditions, for within the lawn, each setback is a step in the direction of a extra colourful and resilient harvest. Happy gardening!

Chapter 12: Advanced Techniques Unveiled

Embarking on the adventure of advanced seed saving techniques is much like moving into the sector of gardening mastery. In this complete guide, we delve into the intricacies of superior seed saving, exploring strategies to save you pass-pollination, saving seeds from hybrids, and pushing the limits with experimental procedures. Elevate your gardening prowess as we remedy the secrets and strategies of superior seed saving.

1. Cross-Pollination Prevention:

a. Understanding Cross-Pollination:

Overview: Cross-pollination happens whilst the pollen from one plant fertilizes the plant life of some different, resulting in seeds with genetic trends from each parent plants.

Challenge: For open-pollinated flora, preserving the genetic purity of seeds may be a venture.

b. Isolation Techniques:

Distance Planting: Separate kinds vulnerable to bypass-pollination with the useful resource of planting them at a extensive distance.

Physical Barriers: Use row covers, mesh baggage, or isolation cages to physical separate plant life, stopping skip-pollination.

c. Timed Planting:

Staggered Planting: Time the planting of various sorts to stagger flowering intervals, decreasing the risk of simultaneous pollination.

Sequential Harvesting: Harvest seeds from every range earlier than the following one starts offevolved offevolved flowering.

d. Hand Pollination:

Selective Pollination: Control the pollination manner by way of way of using hand-pollinating plants. This guarantees targeted fertilization and maintains genetic purity.

Brush Pollination: Use a small brush or cotton swab to replace pollen amongst vegetation, mimicking the herbal pollination device.

2. Hybrid Seed Saving:

a. Understanding Hybrid Plants:

Overview: Hybrid plant life quit end result from the intentional pass-breeding of wonderful figure kinds to offer offspring with specific ideal inclinations.

Challenge: Saving seeds from hybrids does not guarantee proper-to-type vegetation in the subsequent era.

b. Saving Seeds from Hybrids:

Seed Harvesting: Collect seeds from hybrid plants, retaining in thoughts that the offspring might not display off the same tendencies because the decide plant.

Observation and Selection: Grow the hybrid seeds and take a look at the following vegetation. Select people that display favored tendencies for future seed saving.

c. Recreating Hybrids:

Parental Cross-Breeding: If you need to recreate a hybrid, deliberately pass-breed the selected vegetation with the best discern sorts.

Stabilization: Over successive generations, pick out out and keep seeds from plant life that continuously display the famous dispositions, stabilizing the hybrid developments.

3. Experimenting with Advanced Methods:

a. Embarking on Controlled Crosses:

Overview: Delve into the arena of managed crosses, where you intentionally flow awesome kinds to create particular plant combinations.

b. Controlled Cross-Pollination:

Choosing Parent Plants: Select decide plants with particular inclinations you want to mix inside the offspring.

Controlled Pollination: Cover plants with luggage or mesh to save you unwanted pollination. Introduce controlled pollination through the use of hand.

c. Seed Fermentation:

Fermentation Process: Employ fermentation to cut up seeds from the encompassing pulp. This approach is effective for vegetation like tomatoes and cucumbers.

Cleaning and Drying: After fermentation, clean and dry the seeds very well earlier than storage.

d. Embryo Rescue Techniques:

Embryo Extraction: Extract embryos from seeds earlier than they mature definitely.

In Vitro Cultivation: Grow the embryos in a controlled, sterile surroundings, deliberating the improvement of latest plants.

e. Grafting for Seed Production:

Grafting Techniques: Combine superb plant sorts thru grafting, growing a single plant with traits of every.

Seed Saving from Grafted Plants: Collect seeds from grafted vegetation, keeping in thoughts that the following plants might also moreover moreover showcase tendencies from each determine kinds.

Mastering advanced seed saving techniques opens the door to a realm of infinite opportunities on your lawn. Whether preventing pass-pollination, navigating the complexities of hybrid seed saving, or experimenting with managed crosses, those advanced techniques empower you to end up a actual steward of plant genetics.

Embrace the paintings and generation of advanced seed saving, for in your hands lies the potential to create, innovate, and perpetuate a lawn of superb range and splendor. As you challenge into the advanced geographical areas of seed saving, may additionally additionally your lawn thrive with the richness of a tapestry woven with the seeds of your exertions and ingenuity

A Comprehensive Guide to Seed Storage and Organization

As a dedicated gardener and seed saver, the journey does no longer surrender with the harvest. Ensuring the strength and toughness of your seeds is paramount for sustained success. In this big guide, we delve into the art work and technological know-how of seed garage and commercial enterprise commercial enterprise enterprise. From sensible advice on seed garage to putting in place a systematic approach for organizing a numerous seed collection, this guide equips you with the recognise-the way to defend the destiny of your garden.

1. Practical Advice for Seed Storage:

a. Understanding Seed Longevity:

Overview: The toughness of seeds varies, and statistics the elements that effect it's far important for powerful storage.

Factors Affecting Seed Longevity:

Moisture Content: Seeds with low moisture content material material commonly generally tend to have longer shelf lives.

Temperature: Cool and strong temperatures contribute to prolonged seed viability.

Darkness: Exposure to light can cause premature germination in certain seeds.

b. Suitable Containers:

Airtight Containers: Go for airtight containers to save you moisture and air from attractive in the seeds.

Glass or Plastic: Both glass and awesome plastic bins can be appropriate, however make sure they may be easy and dry earlier than use.

Chapter 13: Fundamental Techniques for Retaining Seeds

Life Cycle and Anatomy of Seeds

Discovering a seed's complicated morphology and life cycle is critical to liberate its mysteries. Success in maintaining seeds relies upon for your functionality to free up the mysteries contained in this small packet.

1. Anatomy Revealed:

A seed is a wellspring of lifestyles, now not most effective a latent issue ready to blossom. Explore its anatomy and observe the layers that defend it: the endosperm, the embryo, and the seed coat. Every issue is important to ensuring the destiny plant's survival and germination. Examine the variations in shape among numerous plant species and families to advantage understanding approximately the splendid strategies for maintaining seeds.

2. The Germination Dance:

Explore a seed's lifestyles cycle from germination to maturity. Discover the variables which have an impact on germination, at the side of moderate, temperature, and moisture. Knowing the levels of increase from seedling to flowering plants will let you choose out the fantastic time to reap seeds. Watch as each seed sprouts right into a colorful plant, revealing the dance of existence inside it.

Selecting the Appropriate Seeds

When it includes storing seeds, timing is crucial. Viability and genetic stability are confident while seeds are harvested at the height of adulthood. Let's test the capacity of precisely timing the manner of saving seeds.

1. The Importance of Time:

Timely seed harvesting requires a careful balance. If a seed is planted too early, it might not be really matured; if it's miles planted too past due, it'd lose its viability or absolutely disperse. Examine the distinct markers associated with various plant species; be aware colour shifts, sense dryness, and pay attention the sound of seeds rustling in their pods.

2. Techniques for Harvesting Seeds Specifically:

Every plant own family has first-rate signs for harvesting. Recognize the subtle cues that suggest whilst the time is right, from the huge browning of sunflower heads to the dry pea pods. Explore the world of botanical cues, which include the excellent rustle of seed pods within the breeze or the crinkling of husks that resemble paper within the nightshade family. Gaining expertise inside the ones plant-unique methods ensures an enough yield of feasible seeds.

three. Things to Think About with Annuals and Perennials:

Perennials and annuals have precise rhythms. Perennials have the luxury of many harvests, at the same time as annuals normally complete their lifestyles cycle in a single growing season. Manage the factors about every, comprehending the nuances of at the same time as and a way to build up seeds to optimize their germination capability.

Cleaning and Preparation of Seeds

Cleaning and processing seeds is an crucial level inside the approach of going from lawn to seed bank. The nice and staying energy of stored seeds are stepped forward through this painstaking method, which moreover guarantees the elimination of particles.

1. The Skill of Cleaning:

It's like sprucing gemstones while you easy seeds. Take off the plant fabric, chaff, and detritus to show the actual nature of every seed. Examine numerous cleaning techniques which is probably appropriate to the residences of great seeds, which include winnowing and sifting. Feel the joy of proudly owning a spotless collection that is ready for sharing or storing.

2. Methods of Drying for Maximum Quality:

Seeds want to be thoroughly dried earlier than being stored. Find out how moisture content material impacts mildew growth and degradation and the way important it is. Investigate strategies like desiccants, air drying, or maybe the use of low warmth settings for some seeds. Each technique guarantees the sturdiness of your seed monetary group by way of meeting the particular requirements of numerous plant households.

3. Seed Storage for Prospective Gardens:

Learn the craft of seed storage as you come to the surrender of your seed-saving journey. Recognize the perfect temperature, humidity, and mild publicity for retaining seed viability. Examine the benefits of numerous garage options, such as hermetic jars or paper envelopes, and regulate your technique to the precise desires of each form of seed.

You become a custodian of life's touchy dance inside every seed thru analyzing the nuances of seed anatomy, perfecting the timing of harvesting, and refining you're cleaning and processing strategies. Happy retaining seeds!

Plant circle of relative's attention: leafy veggies and Herbs

Details approximately Leafy Greens Seed Saving

Not excellent are leafy greens a visible banquet for the eyes and palate, but furthermore they provide a manner of keeping their energy for future generations thru manner of shielding their seeds. Let's discover the way to maintain seeds from the ones environmentally fine heroes.

1. Signals of Bolting and Flowering:

When temperatures rise, leafy veggies like spinach, arugula, and lettuce regularly bolt—produce blooms and set seeds. It's crucial to apprehend bolting symptoms and signs and symptoms in case you need to keep seeds.

Observe how the touchy leaves provide manner to the tall flower stalks, indicating that it's time to permit those great vegetation surrender growing.

2. Vigilance and patience:

A sharp eye and a pinch of staying power are desired for saving seeds from leafy vegetables. Let the plant life growth to their best functionality so that the seeds have enough time to mature inside the flowering systems. Keep a near eye at the improvement of the seeds, taking note of any shade or texture adjustments that allow making a decision whilst to acquire them.

3. Suitable Isolation:

A suitable separation protocol is vital to hold the genetic purity of leafy veggies. Different leafy inexperienced cultivars can bypass-pollinate and result in hybridization. To hold the seeds you keep authentic to the dispositions of the determine plant, create bodily obstacles or temporal isolation to save you undesirable mingling.

4. Cleaning Seeds for Small Wonders:

To distinguish leafy inexperienced seeds from the surrounding chaff, they need to be cautiously wiped smooth because of the truth they are regularly tiny and sensitive. Mild winnowing or sifting strategies are quite effective in extracting these microscopic treasures. Consider the first-rate seed structure of every leafy inexperienced and modify your cleaning techniques hence.

Storage Methods for Herb Seeds

Herbs are those fragrant, savory lawn gem stones that beg to be preserved as seeds. Let's have a look at strategies to maintain the essence of your garden's herbs, from the first-rate fragrance of basil to the robust aroma of rosemary.

1. Comprehending the Cycles of Herb Life:

Herbs are a diverse employer of vegetation with biennial, annual, and perennial existence cycles. Learn about the proper existence cycle of every plant, considering the truth that this may assist you select out the terrific time and approach for harvesting seeds. When it involves annual herbs like basil, seed saving commonly takes place after the developing season, while perennial herbs like oregano can produce seeds all three hundred and sixty 5 days round.

2. The Technique of Chopping and Trimming:

Gaining proficiency in pinching and pruning improves the taste of herbs and affects seed yield. Herbs like mint and basil which can be pinched decrease again motive the plant to pay attention its electricity on growing seeds. But keep with caution—prune sparingly to acquire a balance among selling seed output and preserving plant health.

three. Gathering and Desiccating Seeds:

Before being stored, herb seeds need to be very well dried. When seed heads or pods are absolutely advanced, dried, and about to scatter, harvest them. In a vicinity with sufficient air flow, permit the accrued seeds hold to dry. To make sure a hygienic and effective seed series operation, lightly rubbing or tapping the seeds may also help in freeing them from their pods.

4. Ideal Storage Environments:

Creating the precise garage environment is important to retaining the performance of plant seeds. Store the accrued and well-cleaned seeds in a dry, dark, and cool location. Think approximately using little envelopes or airtight boxes, labeling them cautiously for upcoming plantings, or sharing them with precise herb fanatics.

Chapter 14: Plant Circle of Relatives Focus

Common Vegetable Seed Saving Tips

Beyond the immediately yield, reading the technique of seed storage is a few exclusive manner to absolutely understand the functionality of your vegetable lawn. Let's take a look at some beneficial advice for keeping the seeds of common veggies in order that your chosen cultivars live available.

1. Open-Pollinated Superiority:

Choose veggies which is probably open-pollinated first at the identical time as choosing which ones to keep as seeds. According to their genetic composition, the ones cultivars permit spontaneous pollination. This continues your stored seeds actual to the determine plant, which promotes uniformity and stability in your food lawn.

2. Isolation Methodologies:

For plants whose blooms are pollinated by way of using bugs or the wind, use isolation techniques to save you pass-pollination. Timing planting or erecting physical barriers can guide the protection of the seed stock's integrity. The thriller to a a success isolation is knowing how the flora you've got had been given determined directly to pollinate.

three. Being Alert When Harvesting:

When collecting seeds from well-known greens, timing is top. Let end result ripen to complete maturity on the plant to guarantee that the seeds internal have advanced to their most ability. When identifying the right harvesting duration, be aware about versions in coloration, texture, and firmness.

four. Organizing for Achievement:

Often, defensive husks or fleshy end end result surround vegetable seeds. It takes cautious cleansing to put off the seeds from those covers. Methods like soaking (for beans) or fermentation (for tomatoes and cucumbers) assist smash down surrounding particles, which improves cleansing performance.

Reserving Seeds from Different Fruit Species

In addition to supplying a night meal for the eyes and palate, the big fruit deliver additionally holds the promise of future harvests manner to seed saving. Let's have a take a look at the subtleties of preserving fruit seeds from their many types.

1. Delicious Variety:

Fruits offer a captivating type of possibilities for storing seeds because of their severa flavors and textures. Accept the variety placed interior each fruit family, from the acidic flavors of tomatoes to the wet sweetness of watermelons. Acknowledge the specific capabilities of seeds determined in masses of fruit types.

2. Resolving Issues with Pulp and Gel:

The seeds of many culmination, specially tomatoes, are covered in a pulpy gel.

Fermentation is used to interrupt down this gel to extract the ones seeds. To encourage the herbal fermentation system, allow the seeds sit down in their juices. After fermentation, ensure the seeds are nicely wiped smooth and rinsed to eliminate any leftover pulp.

3. Suitable Drying Methods:

One of the maximum critical steps in shielding fruit seeds is drying. To keep away from mould or degradation, well dry the seeds in advance than storing them. On a non-stick floor, distribute the seeds in a unmarried layer and make certain there's ok airflow for the drying system. For the wonderful drying conditions, fantastic fruit sorts can also require specific troubles.

four. How to Store Fruit Seeds:

Fruit seeds' energy is considerably dependent on the garage conditions. Seeds must be saved in a dry, dark, and funky place—preferably in sealed bags or hermetic bins.

Make certain to cautiously label every box with the fruit kind and the accumulating date. This meticulous interest to detail ensures well-prepared and wholesome seed assets for upcoming plantings.

Savor the specific flavors and textures of every species as you acquire down to maintain the seeds from common forestall end result and vegetables. Your garden becomes a residing archive of numerous, locally grown delights genuinely ready to be sowed once more, similarly to being a source of right now meals. Happy saving seeds on your bountiful lawn!

Plant own family consciousness: ornamental and floral

Investigating Seed Preservation in Decorative Plants

In addition to their adorable visible enchantment, ornamental vegetation gift a compelling threat for seed saving, which lets in you to preserve the beauty of your lawn.

Now allow's explore the special capabilities of saving seeds from ornamental plants.

1. Different Families of Ornaments:

There are many precise families of ornamental plant life, ranging from colourful annuals like marigolds and zinnias to super perennials like roses and lilies. Successful seed saving calls for an know-how of the existence cycles and seed shape of those numerous households. Explore the arena of ornamental range and observe the extraordinary trends that set each plant aside as a garden treasure.

2. Gathering Seeds for Visual Appeal:

Take beneath interest the seen appeal of beautiful flowers and their seeds whilst retaining their seeds. Select seeds from the healthiest, happiest, and maximum actual-to-kind specimens to preserve the famous traits. Make effective the seeds internal are absolutely formed with the aid of manner of accumulating the seeds after the blossoms have grown and the seed heads or pods have dried.

three. Methods for Drying Decorative Seeds:

The maintenance of attractive seeds requires careful drying. Allow seeds to air dry certainly, being cautious no longer to harm their sensitive architecture. Examine the particular drying desires of various decorative plant life, preserving in thoughts that some can also moreover need close to attention to keep away from unfavourable the seeds or dropping viability.

4. Keeping Genetic Purity Alive:

Beautiful gardens frequently function an array of colours and shapes. Use isolation strategies to maintain appealing plant life genetically herbal. Hybrids can upward push up even as one in all a type kinds inside the equal family move-pollinate. Prevent unwanted genetic combinations to maintain the integrity of your desired decorative kinds.

Preserving Your Garden's Beauty

By extending the life and legacy of your prized decorative plant life, you may lengthen their beauty and add a fulfilling touch to your lawn. Let's have a study a few techniques for maintaining the beauty and glide of your garden's layout.

1. Creating a Successor Design:

When designing your garden, remember the future. When designing with succession in thoughts, one have to carefully don't forget while and wherein to region decorative vegetation that bloom and set seeds at a few level within the 12 months. This ensures a normal show of beauty and gives masses of possibilities to keep seeds all year prolonged.

2. Conscientious Gathering:

It takes finesse to gain seeds from ornamental plants. Pick a time at the same time as the plant's seed heads or pods have glaringly dried. Take warning in the course of harvesting, making sure to accumulate seeds on the fullest ripeness. Think approximately how your lawn panorama will appearance if you go away a few seed heads for winter appeal.

3. Storage of Seeds as a Time Capsule:

Ornamental plant seeds may be preserved like a time tablet, bringing another time the splendor of first-class garden moments. Create a carefully chosen series of seeds and label them to hold them for destiny use in making breathtaking suggests on your garden. Store the seeds in a groovy, dry spot.

four. Spreading the Beauty:

Not quality are you able to maintain the splendor of your garden with seed upkeep from decorative plant life, however you could moreover percentage it with others. Take under attention giving seeds to different lawn fans or taking thing in seed exchanges. You add to the bigger cloth of horticulture pleasure thru sharing the splendor you have grown.

Your lawn can come to be a residing, respiratory paintings of paintings that is conserved through the usage of seeds if you take at the captivating route of preserving seeds from appealing vegetation. Every blossom and seed pod can inform an aesthetically stunning story within the ensuing seasons. Happy storing seeds in your garden retreat!

Advance Seed Saving technique

Cross-Pollination and Isolation Methods

Preserving the purity of seed versions requires navigating the complex dance of bypass-pollination. Let's take a look at skip-pollination dynamics and realistic isolation strategies to protect your plant life' genetic integrity.

1. Knowing How to Cross-Pollinate:

When pollen from one plant fertilizes the blooms of every other, a method known as skip-pollination takes region that might bring about hybridization. Find out how your plants are pollinated, together with in the event that they rely upon bugs, the wind, or different assets. The foundation for putting into exercising a hit isolation processes is that this information.

2. Methods of Spatial Isolation:

Plants need to be physical separated to keep away from circulate-pollination. This may also entail carefully setting vegetation aside to lessen the possibility of pollen switch. Take into consideration the unique wishes of each plant family and adjust spacing regular with the pollination techniques used by your preferred cultivars.

3. Strategies for Temporal Isolation:

Reduce the danger of pass-pollination via using way of controlling the date of flowering. To avoid plant overlap due to comparable flowering intervals, this may entail staggered planting timings. For flora that bloom asynchronously or with extended flowering seasons, temporal separation could be very critical.

four. Applying Barriers:

Pollen may be correctly stopped from moving from one plant to a few different with the beneficial useful resource of bodily barriers. One can use techniques like bagging precise blooms or entire plant life. Controlled pollination and seed development are made feasible thru the protecting protect supplied with the aid of mesh baggage or specialized isolation cages.

5. Pollination through way of using hand for regulated crosses:

If stylish isolation proves to be hard, reflect onconsideration on hand pollination as a way of dealing with the breeding method. Hand-transfer pollen from one plant to every different, taking care to control the proper crossings and hold genetic integrity. This method works mainly properly for plants with complex floral systems.

Handling Transient Plants

Because of their -12 months life cycle, biennial flora provide particular barriers further to opportunities for storing seeds. Now allow's check some practical techniques for handling biennial flowers approximately seed saving.

1. Recognizing the Cycle of Biennials:

In their first 12 months, biennial plants broaden vegetatively, and of their second one year, they start to generate seeds. Comprehending this cycle is important to organizing and sporting out powerful seed-saving procedures. To begin flowering, biennials often want a duration of vernalization—exposure to bloodless temperatures.

2. Winterizing Methods:

Plants need to be well overwintered to effectively maintain seeds from biennials. This regularly includes giving the flowers sufficient cooling hours and protecting them from harsh wintry weather weather. Biennials can be included from iciness damage via way of mulching and imparting refuge.

three. Keeping an eye fixed out for bolting:

In their 2nd 365 days, biennials generally tend to bolt and bring flora. Pay cautious interest on your biennial flora as they skip from vegetative increase to the reproductive diploma. Identify the symptoms of bolting, which encompass stem extension and the onset of flower buds.

four. Gathering Seeds for the Next Year:

When biennial flora attain the flowering degree of their 2nd 12 months, it surely is whilst the seeds are harvested. After the seed heads or pods have grown and dried, permit the flora end their life cycle and then gather the seeds. For seeds to be possible and mature, timing is important.

five. Rotating Your Crops to Prevent Diseases:

Certain illnesses can have an impact on biennial plant life and show signs and symptoms and symptoms in some unspecified time inside the future in their -three hundred and sixty five days existence cycle. By putting into practice a crop rotation approach, sickness accumulation within the soil can be avoided, resulting in more healthful vegetation and stronger seed materials.

Gaining an interest of the unique difficulties confronted through biennial vegetation, in addition to the complexities of move-pollination dynamics and the usage of green isolation strategies, will enable you to take charge of seed-saving techniques with care. Cheers to storing seeds and exploring the brilliant realm of plant life cycles and replica!

Chapter 15: Troubleshooting and Common Mistakes

Determining and Resolving Seed Preservation Issues

Starting a seed-saving adventure has its percentage of problems, however the ones may be avoided with cautious planning and observation. Let's check trendy boundaries to seed saving and viable answers:

1. Concerns approximately Cross-Pollination:

Difficulty: Unintentional hybridization due to skip-pollination can jeopardize the integrity of preserved seeds.

Overcoming the Challenge: Use isolation strategies to stop cross-pollination, collectively with temporal, geographical, or physical obstacles. Considering the proper necessities of your plants, pick suitable strategies.

2. Management of Diseases:

Difficulty: Plant and seed illnesses would possibly probably have an effect at the viability of the seeds.

Overcoming the Challenge: Maintain a smooth and illness-unfastened environment in your lawn through working closer to properly hygiene. Select ailment-resistant cultivars, rotate your plants, and most effective acquire seeds from sturdy plant life.

three. Insect Pests Affecting the Quality of Seed:

Difficulty: Insect pests have the capability to harm seedlings or spread contamination.

Overcoming the Challenge: Regularly check plant life for pests, employ herbal pest control techniques, and rent herbal predators. Gather seeds as quickly as viable to reduce pest harm.

4. Early Harvesting of Seeds:

Difficulty: Seeds which can be harvested too quickly may not turn into fertile seeds.

Overcoming the Difficulty: Permit seeds to gain complete adulthood at the plant. Before harvesting, maintain a watch regular out for signs and signs and symptoms unique to each plant type, along with color adjustments and dryness.

five. Insufficient Desiccation:

Difficulty: Mold and reduced viability of seeds may additionally end result from insufficient drying.

Taking up the Challenge: Make super everything dries honestly in advance than storing. Ensure ok air circulation while dispensing seeds in a single layer. Adapt drying strategies to the seeds' period and shape.

6. Examining the Conditions of Seed Storage:

Difficulty: Seed degradation may additionally additionally cease end end result from wrong garage situations.

Overcoming the Difficulty: Keep seeds in cold, dry, and darkish places. Seeds need to be saved dry and free of insects with the aid of being saved in sealed luggage or hermetic packing containers. Put crucial records on the labels of the bins.

7. Insufficient Genetic Variety:

Problem: Preserving seeds from a small form of vegetation over the years can also bring about a decrease in genetic variety.

Overcoming the Challenge: Consistently introduce new sorts, each thru buying seeds or changing them. This makes high-quality that your lawn's gene pool is certainly one of a type, which evokes resilience.

Recognizing Typical Errors

Every gardener has limitations to conquer and errors to make. Gaining records from these encounters is critical to emerge as an expert seed saver. Here are some ordinary mistakes and insightful insights:

1. Plant Identification Ignored:

Error: Inaccurate plant range identity also can reason confusion and incorrectly categorised seeds.

Takeaway: Carefully label your plant life, noting their kind, planting date, and a few other pertinent info. Spend a while reading the trends of flowers to make sure particular identity.

2. Ignoring to Keep Records:

Error: It is tough to display screen the effectiveness of seed-saving tasks while whole statistics are not maintained.

Takeaway: Record planting dates, seed assets, and any observations in a lawn pocket ebook. Keep song of your victories and setbacks to decorate your seed-saving strategies.

3. Looking Over the Local Climate:

Error: Ignoring the precise weather in your region ought to bring about insufficient seed adaption.

Lesson: Choose plant types suitable for the weather to your location. For powerful seed saving, be aware of the particular requirements that flora on your location have.

four. Hastily Going Through the Process:

Error: Rushing the harvest and processing of seeds may additionally bring about underripe or low-brilliant seeds.

Teaching second: Be affected individual at the same time as preserving seeds. Let seeds collect entire maturity and make the effort with regards to accurate harvesting and cleaning techniques.

five. Ignoring the Testing of Seed Viability:

Error: Planting non-feasible seeds can be the impact of failing to assess seed viability.

Lesson: Use germination assays to periodically verify the viability of stored seeds. By doing this, you may plant seeds that have the tremendous danger of germinating efficiently.

6. Plant Genetics Ignored:

Error: Preserving seeds with out taking plant genetics into consideration also can want to result in undesired talents in next generations.

Lesson: Study the homes and genetics of plants. Select flora which have the tendencies you need to your garden while maintaining seeds.

7. Underestimating the Need for Space:

Error: Cross-pollination can occur even as flowers' location requirements are disregarded.

Lesson: Find out how masses place flora which might be liable to skip-pollination need. Use isolation techniques effectively to preserve the purity of your seed.

Your seed-saving skills are extra with the aid of recognizing boundaries, drawing close to them strategically, and selecting up classes from past mistakes. Every setback will become a gaining knowledge of possibility that lets in you expand a greater resilient and fruitful seed-saving everyday for your garden. Happy retaining seeds!

Preserving Biodiversity and Heirloom Varieties

Seed Saving's Significance for Biodiversity

Saving seeds is crucial for preserving biodiversity, bolstering surroundings resilience, and making sure the lengthy-time period viability of agriculture. Now permit's discover the numerous strategies that seed saving contributes to and maintains biodiversity:

1. Conserving Different Plant Types:

Benefit to Biodiversity: By keeping some of plant kinds, which encompass nearby species and heirlooms, seed renovation allows prevent the dearth of genetic variety inside plant organizations.

How it Works: Gardeners can aid inside the safety of super trends, adaptability, and resilience that various cultivars offer to the environment with the resource of the usage of storing seeds from hundreds of plant life.

2. Adjusting to Shifts within the Environment:

Benefit to Biodiversity: A severa seed monetary institution allows reaction to shifting environmental factors, in conjunction with changes in climate and the emergence of latest pests or ailments.

How it Works: Plants with seeds preserved have genetic tendencies which could provide resistance to environmental stresses. This ability to comply is vital to a plant's functionality to continue to exist unexpected obstacles.

three. Promoting the habitats of pollinators:

Biological Benefit: A form of blooming plants made viable through seed-saving obligations offer pollinators a desire of habitats, which enhances the properly-being of bee, butterfly, and outstanding pollinator populations.

How it Works: To produce a consistent deliver of pollen and nectar, seed savers frequently expand a aggregate of plant life with diverse flowering seasons. A thriving community of pollinators is supported via this diverse floral habitat.

four. Promoting Interactions Among Ecosystems:

Benefit to Biodiversity: A big style of plant species encourage complicated interactions among creatures in ecosystems, maintaining everything from tiny soil bacteria to massive mammals.

How it Works: The lifestyles of numerous flowers in a certain place is facilitated with the aid of seed-saving strategies. Different organisms are interested by this variety, which creates complex ecological linkages that enhance the fitness of the surroundings as an entire.

five. Boosting Regional Agriculture:

Benefit to Biodiversity: By encouraging the adoption of locally appropriate plant kinds, seed conservation will increase agricultural range and lessens reliance on a small large kind of business seed types.

How it Works: Local seed-saving packages promote the increase of domestically tailored cultivars, preserving traditional data and permitting farmers to select flowers suitable for his or her precise place.

Traditional Seeds and Their Significance

Heritage seeds—additionally known as heirloom seeds—have genetic, historical, and cultural charge. The story of seed saving and biodiversity maintenance advantages from an information of the significance of ancient beyond seeds.

1. Preservation of Cultural Heritage:

Importance: Legacy seeds hold a network's past and cultural price via the use of being surpassed down via the generations.

How it Works: Gardeners assist keep cultural traditions, culinary customs, and anecdotes associated with those plant life via manner of preserving and dispersing ancient past seeds.

2. Conservation of Genetic Diversity:

Importance: Heritage seeds regularly have specific genetic abilties and variations that may be misplaced in traditional farming.

How it Works: Heritage seeds make a contribution to genetic range conservation through way of serving as a storehouse of abilties that could be beneficial for upcoming breeding responsibilities when planted in seed banks and gardens.

three. Promoting Sovereignty of Seeds:

Importance: Heritage seeds assist network manage over their seed resources via the usage of selling seed sovereignty.

How it Works: Promoting the trade and use of heritage seeds enables network seed producers turn out to be greater independent through reducing their reliance on out of doors seed resources.

four. Adaptability in Changing Environments:

Importance: Heritage seeds can also very very own trends that allow them to thrive particularly regions, improving agricultural resilience in opposition to climate exchange.

How it Works: Resilience in agriculture and meals structures can be accelerated by using manner of using cultivating and retaining seeds from historical past sorts that have been appropriate to close through conditions.

five. Honoring Diversity in Culinary Arts:

Importance: Heritage seeds help maintain specific tastes, textures, and cooking customs related to exceptional plant species.

Chapter 16: Community and Global Impact

Spreading Seeds Both Locally and Worldwide

Sharing seeds creates links between gardeners, allows biodiversity, and offers to a international seed upkeep life-style beyond country wide borders. Let's study the importance of dispersing seeds regionally and global:

1. Local Exchange of Seeds:

Importance: By encouraging the boom of flowers suitable to high-quality climates and environments, local seed exchanges strengthen agencies' resilience.

How it Works: By changing seeds which might be suitable for their precise climate, gardeners inspire the development of hardy and locally tailored plant species. This encourages self-sufficiency and fortifies nearby meals systems.

2. Worldwide Seed Exchange:

Importance: International seed exchanges permit one-of-a-kind plant kinds to be shared, which promotes biodiversity on a bigger scale.

How it Works: Seed aficionados community globally, trading seeds that won't be effects determined in their regions. The sharing of agricultural and cultural traditions in addition to the renovation of uncommon genetic assets are blessings of this global alternate.

3. Sustaining Genetic Variability:

Importance: Local or international seed exchanges are critical for preserving genetic range in plant populations.

How it Works: Gardeners assist keep wonderful competencies and variations with the useful resource of spreading the gene pool thru seed exchanges. Both the sustainability of agriculture and the resilience of ecosystems rely on this genetic range.

4. Encouraging Regional Agriculture:

Importance: By encouraging the usage of domestically tailored cultivars and bolstering seed sovereignty, seed sharing allows neighborhood farmers and gardeners.

How it Works: Local seed exchanges amongst farmers and gardeners promote the boom of flora which might be properly-tailor-made to network situations. This in flip encourages sustainable farming strategies and strengthens the resilience of close by agriculture.

5. Collaboration and Cultural Exchange:

Importance: As gardeners percentage not simplest seeds but moreover the legends, customs, and facts related to the ones seeds, sharing seeds promotes move-cultural trade.

How it Works: By taking component in exchanges and swaps of seeds, human beings participate in a far wider cultural communication, sharing expertise and honoring the tremendous variety of the arena's plant historic past.

Participating in Conservation and Seed Exchanges

Initiatives for conservation and seed exchanges are colourful representations of community efforts to guard biodiversity and guarantee quite some plant species for coming generations:

1. Local Exchanges of Seeds:

Proactive: Engage in community seed exchanges or begin one for your area.

Impact: Local seed exchanges offer gardeners a danger to percentage seeds, know-how, and recommendation. This encourages network biodiversity and fortifies ties within the network.

2. Online Exchanges for Seeds:

Project: Investigate web websites that facilitate seed exchanges and connect to on-line agencies of seed savers.

Impact: Global connections made viable by manner of manner of online seed exchanges supply people get proper of access to to a big fashion of plant species. This enables hold some of seeds and promotes a experience of global network.

three. Contributions from Seed Banks:

Project: Participate in community seed banks or donate seeds to seed banks.

Impact: Genetic variety is saved in seed banks. By donating seeds, you may make certain the availability of a large type of plant species with the useful resource of protective these assets for later use.

four. Partnerships for Conservation:

Initiative: Assist neighborhood botanical gardens or conservation organizations in their efforts to maintain seeds.

Impact: Collaborating with conservation tasks allows big campaigns aimed towards maintaining unusual or endangered plant species. This cooperative method increases the overall effect of seed-saving tasks.

five. Outreach in Education:

Project: Promote conservation and seed saving thru instructional outreach.

Impact: Spreading recognition of conservation and seed saving encourages humans to get worried in those responsibilities. A robust sense of duty and interest-elevating for biodiversity can be fostered thru schooling.

People who percentage seeds each domestically and internationally, take part in seed exchanges, and artwork closer to conservation upload to a colourful and interwoven global community of seed savers. Our plant legacy will continue to be enough and resilient because to the coordinated efforts of sustainable agriculture, cultural trade, and biodiversity conservation. Happy route of conservation and seed sharing!

CONCLUSION

Examining Your Experience with Seed Saving

Take a minute to bear in mind your journey of preserving seeds as you stand amid the inexperienced tapestry of your lawn, every plant serving as a witness to the cycles of life and the revolutionary splendor of nature. Think approximately the seeds you're keeping; every one bears witness to your willpower, situation, and the dance of life which you have tended. The following reflections can help you with yourself-exam:

1. Life Stewardship:

Thought: By retaining seeds, you've got were given assumed the stewardship characteristic and been entrusted with the safety of lifestyles cycles. Your deeds bring a seasonal resonance, connecting preceding harvests to imminent blossoms.

Think: In what techniques can preserving seeds red meat up your bond with the living world spherical you?

2. Uncovering the Wisdom of Nature:

Thought: The complicated patterns and rhythms of nature have served as your mentor. Every seed conveys a story of flexibility, tenacity, and the knowledge innate in the approach of pollination and development.

Think: What insights regarding the resiliency and intelligence woven at some degree within the material of nature has your experience saving seeds determined out?

three. The Generations You Hold:

Thought: Every seed you shop has the functionality to produce many generations of plant life in the future. Your palms preserve botanical legacies and characteristic a hyperlink some of the beyond and the future.

Think: How does your standpoint at the changing of the seasons change because of your responsibility as a father or mother of genetic historical beyond?

four. Diversity as Plenty:

Thought: The various fabric of life is contemplated on your lawn, that may be a patchwork of hues, styles, and tastes. Your brushstroke has been saving seeds, at the side of layers to this enormous canvas.

Think: How has your enjoy as a seed saver and nurturer been more appropriate through embracing variety on your lawn?

Suggested Path for Further Research

Allow the sound of birdsong overhead and the whispering of the wind via the foliage to accompany you for your journey as you hold learning about seed garage. Here's a hint consolation for the adventure ahead:

1. Accept Curiosity:

Inspiration: Embrace your interest as you test out novel plant species, techniques, and the constantly unraveling enigmas surrounding the field of seed preserving. There's constantly some aspect sparkling to find out with each season.

Think: How could likely developing a spirit of inquiry improve your dating with the changing narratives to your lawn?

2. Honor your imperfections:

Inspiration: Flaws are a essential thing of splendor in the dance of nature. Honor the peculiarities, the surprising intersections, and the revelations that nature bestows upon each seed.

Think: How can also moreover accepting flaws assist you recognize how unique each seed and plant is?

three. Distribute the Harvest:

Inspiration: Share seeds with exclusive gardeners to unfold the pride of your seed-saving adventure. Like memories, seeds come to existence while they will be shared.

www.ingramcontent.com/pod-product-compliance
Lightning Source LLC
Chambersburg PA
CBHW071446080526
44587CB00014B/2013